SEMEIA 47

Interpretation for Liberation

Katie Geneva Cannon, Guest Editor

Elisabeth Schüssler Fiorenza, Editor

© 1989
by the Society of Biblical Literature

SEMEIA 47

Copyright © 1989 by the Society of Biblical Literature

All rights reserved. No part of this work may be reproduced or transmitted in any form or by any means, electronic or mechanical, including photocopying and recording, or by means of any information storage or retrieval system, except as may be expressly permitted by the 1976 Copyright Act or in writing from the publisher. Requests for permission should be addressed in writing to the Rights and Permissions Office, Society of Biblical Literature, 825 Houston Mill Road, Atlanta, GA 30329, USA.

ISSN 0095-571X
ISBN 1-58983-067-9

Printed in the United States of America
on acid-free paper

CONTENTS

Contributors to This Issue   iv

Introduction
Elisabeth Schüssler Fiorenza   1

I.   Slave Ideology and Biblical Interpretation
Katie Geneva Cannon   9

II.   Discovering the Bible in the Non-Biblical World
Kwok Pui Lan   25

III.   Historical/Cultural Criticism as Liberation.
A Proposal for an African American Biblical Hermeneutic
Vincent L. Wimbush   43

IV.   "Mother to the Motherless, Father to the Fatherless:"
Power, Gender, and Community in Afrocentric Biblical
Tradition
Cheryl Townsend Gilkes   57

V.   Gomer: Victim of Violence or Victim of Metaphor
Renita Weems   87

VI.   A Chamberlain's Journey and the Challenge of
Interpretation for Liberation
Clarice J. Martin   105

VII.   Can an Enslaved God Liberate? Hermeneutical
Reflections on Philippians 2:6-11
Sheila Briggs   137

CONTRIBUTORS TO THIS ISSUE

Sheila Briggs
Department of Religion
University of Southern California
328 Taper Hall of Humanities
Los Angeles, CA 90089-0355

Katie Geneva Cannon
Episcopal Divinity School
99 Brattle Street
Cambridge, MA 02138

Cheryl Townsend Gilkes
Department of Sociology and Anthropology
Colby College
Waterville, ME 04901

Kwok Pui Lan
Theology Building
Chung Chi College
Chinese University of Hong Kong
Sharton, N.T.
Hong Kong

Clarice J. Martin
Princeton Theological Seminary
CN 821
Princeton, NJ 08542

Elisabeth Schüssler Fiorenza
Harvard Divinity School
45 Francis Avenue
Cambridge, MA 02138

Renita J. Weems
Vanderbilt Divinity School
Vanderbilt University
Nashville, TN 37240

Vincent L. Wimbush
Claremont School of Theology
1325 N. College Avenue
Claremont, CA 91711

INTRODUCTION

Elisabeth Schüssler Fiorenza
Harvard Divinity School

The essays in this issue of *Semeia* are different. They do not focus either on the discussion of a new literary critical method, nor on the introduction of sociological or anthropological theories, nor on the exploration of a certain biblical book or theological topic. Neither Bultmann nor Albright, Troeltsch nor Geertz, Derrida nor Foucault are their exegetical or theoretical "Godfathers". Rather they speak from social contexts, hermeneutical points of view, and theological interests quite different from those of Euro-American Christian biblical scholarship.

Nevertheless, they share the theoretical interests which have emerged across academic disciplines in discourses of resistance. Such so-called "minority discourses" have been generated by those who are marginalized in academy and society but who in fact constitute the majority--women of all colours and men exploited by racism, classism, and colonialism (Abdul R. JanMohamed and David Lloyd, 1987). Their critique of universal White Western Man (e.g. Judith Newton and Deborah Rosenfelt, 1985; Teresa de Lauretis, 1987, or Seyla Benhabib and Drucilla Cornell, 1987), their use of race, gender, and class as meaningful analytical categories (e.g. Henry Louis Gates, Jr., 1986; Martin Bernal, 1987; Marjorie Pryse and Hortense J. Spillers, 1985), as well as their insistence on discourses as strategies of power and subjection (e.g. Edward Said, 1978; Chris Weedon, 1987; Tory Yuge and Masaoki Doi, 1988).

The writers of these essays are all young scholars who in various ways seek to fashion new models and approaches for a Christian biblical interpretation that could support people's struggle for justice, self-determination and freedom. With the exception of Vincent Wimbush and myself all other contributors speak from the experience of double marginalization. As Afro-American or Asian women scholars they are a tiny minority in the white male Euro-American academy not only because of their race or culture but also because of their gender. They are the quintessential Other in the dominant white male academy.

The idea for this volume germinated in a course on New Testament and Ethics which Professor Cannon and I team-taught from a womanist and feminist liberation theological perspective. Since at the same time I was invited to the *Semeia* editorial board in order to plan an issue on feminist or liberation theology, we decided that this issue should not be about a biblical hermeneutics of liberation alone but should bring together scholars who are a marginal minority in biblical studies. We had hoped to include other contributions by Asian-, Hispanic-, Afro-, and Native American women and men in this collection, but we were not successful in soliciting them. This is partly due to our own social-racial location but mostly reflects the dearth of such scholars in biblical studies. Kwok Pui Lan's is the only voice that is not Afro-American. Her essay highlights not only the global-cultural but also the pluralistic-religious contexts of biblical interpretation.

Contributors approach the topic from two distinct directions. The first set of articles theoretically elaborate principles and models for biblical interpretation. Co-editor Katie Cannon opens the discourse on the hermeneutics of liberation by naming racial slavery as the socio-political context of biblical interpretation. As an ethicist she asks what kind of socio-ethical values and symbolic constructs have enabled the dominant white Christian church and academy to justify chattel slavery biblically and theologically. She identifies three such ideological religious constructs: As *property* black slaves were declared not to be fully human; as *Africans* they were classed as superstitious heathen savages to be christianized and saved by enslavement; and finally, as *Christians*, white or black, they were to believe that the institution of slavery was willed by God and divinely revealed in the bible. One of the major arguments insists that the institution of slavery is taken for granted in the bible. Neither Christ nor the apostles objected to it, for enslavement to sin is an offence in the order of salvation, whereas slavery as an institution is a part of the natural order of creation.

Cannon's historical-systemic analysis graphically highlights how much dominant hermeneutical frameworks of biblical interpretation are determined by economic, institutional, cultural and racial interests. A hermeneutics of suspicion is therefore called for! Such a hermeneutics can identify and make explicit the institutional patriarchal interests that seek to sustain dehumanizing racism, economic, and cultural superiority of Euro-Americans, and the exploitation of all women but especially of those who are not only oppressed by sexism but also by racism, poverty, and colonialism. However, just as the legitimization of slavery has determined the biblical readings of the white churches, so also the experience of slavery has shaped Afro-American biblical interpretation. It is the critical principle that allows for an ethical evaluation of biblical texts (C. West, 1988).

The contribution of Kwok Pui Lan is not situated in the North-American but in a global cultural and different religious context. It focuses on the political colonialist implications of biblical interpretation, and is written explicitly from a Chinese woman's perspective. Reading the bible in a non-Christian world, Asian Christians question both whether the biblical canon contains all the truth and whether it is rigidly closed. They challenge the universal truth-claims of Western biblical interpretation and judge the authority and meaningfulness of the bible not on philosophical-theological grounds but measure it by the praxis of the Christian community. For interpreting the bible in a global religiously pluralistic context Kwok Pui Lan proposes a process of "dialogical imagination" as a new hermeneutical model derived from Asian theological reflection. Such a model uses Asian cultural and religious traditions and texts for biblical reflection as well as the social biography of the people as a hermeneutical key for biblical interpretation.

Vincent Wimbush too advocates a culture-specific interpretation of the bible. Like Katie Cannon, Wimbush is rooted in the black church. However, his contribution does not seek to debunk the dominant use of the bible for justifying the dehumanization of black people. Rather he argues that Afro-Americans consciously should utilize for their own purposes the historical-critical and cultural-critical scholarship on the bible which the white Euro-American academy has developed over and against the dogmatic control of the dominant churches.

Wimbush's starting point is the theological dilemma of the black church which was founded in response to the socio-religious needs of Afro-Americans but often has embraced uncritically the confessional frameworks and literalist fundamentalism of the dominant white Euro-American churches. Therefore, he argues that the historical-critical study of religions in general and of biblical traditions in particular is potentially liberating for oppressed peoples and can serve to distance the black church from the dominant hermeneutical constructs. However, such a historical-critical hermeneutic must be complemented by a cross-cultural analysis that can determine which symbols and referents of biblical and contemporary cultures are relevant for a positive self-understanding of Afro-Americans as a people with a heritage and a future.

Whereas Wimbush seeks to utilize the historical- and cultural-critical methods of white academic scholarship for Afro-American biblical interpretation, Cheryl Townsend Gilkes highlights the Afrocentric strategies which the black church developed for utilizing biblical texts. In distinction to the previous articles she does not elaborate an Afrocentric biblical hermeneutics in general. Rather she concretely elucidates with reference to a short phrase in Ps 68:5 how Afrocentric biblical interpretation expands and elaborates on certain biblical phrases and motives in order to shape a religious Christian tradition appropriate to the situation of the black community. Townsend Gilkes shows that the African-American tradition contains a critical moment that allows the black community to use and transform biblical texts for its own purposes. Her contribution sheds a different light on Wimbush's contention that the black church often subscribes to a literalist fundamentalism which is pre-critical.

Townsend Gilke's contribution forms a bridge to the second set of articles in this collection that seek to elaborate interpretive models for a biblical hermeneutics of liberation by focusing on the interpretation of particular texts. Renita Weems engages in a close reading of Hos 2:4-25 by paying careful attention to the image of sexual violence in the judgment speeches. She argues that the marriage metaphor functions in three ways in this text: This metaphor articulates the sexual violence which makes Gomer a pawn in the match between Hosea (YHWH) and her lovers (other Gods). Further, it underscores that punishment must be meted out before reconciliation is possible, and finally, it functions as a poetic device to relate the punishment to the crime.

Although Weems applauds the poetic versatility of the marriage metaphor for expressing a wide range of female sexual experiences and for stressing the intimacy and love of the covenant-relationship, she nevertheless does not overlook the serious hermeneutical and theological problems it presents. Utilizing insights from Sally McFague's metaphorical theology she cautions biblical readers against oversimplification of such metaphors and against the assumption of rigid correspondence between religious language and the Divine.

Like Townsend Gilkes she is aware that a hermeneutical critique of such biblical texts and metaphors is present in the black community but she contends that this critique does not challenge biblical authority. Weems is hesitant to reject explicitly the authority of this biblical text that promotes violence and oppression--as I have argued in my own work (Schüssler Fiorenza, 1984) a critical feminist hermeneutics of liberation must do. Instead she employs the categories of analogy and metaphor in order to transform such violent language for authorization in the liberation struggle. Her hesitancy to face the problem head on, at first glance seems to support Wimbush's contention that black churches often have internalized dominant white biblicism. However, Weems' hesitancy could also be understood as rooted in the knowledge that those without power and authority cannot afford to relinquish lightly any authorizing resource and heritage in the struggle for survival, freedom and dignity (Katie Cannon, 1985).

Clarice Martin in contrast does not analyze an oppressive biblical text. Rather she utilizes and expands a feminist hermeneutics of suspicion in order to retrieve the New Testament story of a black African convert to Christianity as a culturally affirming and empowering tradition. She documents the "politics of omission" at work in scholarly interpretations of the Ethiopian official's conversion (Acts 8:26-40). While stressing the theological motifs and significance of this story, exegetes have downplayed or denied the significance of the Ethiopian's ethnic identity by refusing to identify Ethiopians as black-skinned people. They have neglected to inform readers that in the Greco-Roman world "Ethiopian" was used as a generic term for denoting dark-skinned peoples as well as that Ethiopia was one of the four geographical areas denoting "the ends of the earth" (cf. Acts 1:8). Martin points out that Euro-American New Testament scholarship shares this "politics of omission" and marginalization with the treatment of "blacks" or "black Africans" in classical scholarship. Frank Snowden (1979) and more recently Martin Bernal (1987) have highlighted how much racist assumptions have permeated the scholarly study of the classical world in the last 200 years.

Sheila Briggs also is concerned with a hermeneutics of reconstruction but addresses a different set of problems. Unlike Martin she does not analyze biblical interpretations and reconstructions offered by white dominant scholarship. Instead she seeks to explore the role of analogy in historical reconstruction and its hermeneutical implications for the oppressed. By drawing an analogy between the social relationships of oppression and liberation in the past and in the present she seeks to understand the metaphor of the enslavement of Christ in the pre-Pauline hymn Phil 2:6-11 by means of two sets of categories developed in the work of Orlando Patterson.

She argues that the stress on the freely chosen enslavement of Christ and his obedience communicated to the slaves on the one hand that they are essentially not slaves but on the other hand that in obedience they should not resist their enslavement. Although the identification of Christ with God could have given subversive power to the text in the imagination and subjectivity of Christian slaves, this subversive potential of the text was muted because human beings could not like Christ choose their servile status. However, the tension in the text, Briggs argues, made it possible for Christian slaves to subvert the text insofar as the enslavement of God in Christ made an inversion of the hierarchy of being and worth possible.

Briggs constructs as historical "subtext" to the text the mentality of ancient slave-society in which the abolition of the social institution of slavery was inconceivable to both freeborn and slaves. One wonders how the text would read if as its historical "subtext" the Christian community rather than society at large would be reconstructed since we have indications that some Jewish and Christian communities did not condone institutional slavery in their own midst (Schüssler Fiorenza, 1983; Norman Petersen, 1985).

In conclusion: Utilizing quite different historical-literary critical methods and theoretical models of interpretation, these analyses nevertheless articulate common insights and critical challenges that white Euro-American biblical scholarship no longer can disregard. The authors highlight the colonialist contexts and racial rhetoric of biblical scholarship. They draw our attention to the biased readings and reconstructions of exegetes who claim to be objective and scientific. Committed to the liberation struggle and rooted in the Christian community they prove that an "interested" reading of biblical texts is not less scholarly and historically adequate. To the contrary, it is more able to do justice to the rich dimensions of biblical texts and their socio-historical contexts. Rather than advocating value-free scholarship they require a public articulation of scholarly values and commitments (Schüssler Fiorenza, 1988). They draw their critical intellectual force not from intellectual rationalism or academic anti-dogmatism but from their commitment to the liberation struggle of their people. What the poet June Jordan says about black poetry thus applies equally to a biblical liberation hermeneutics and theology:

> Our art does not arise from the academy, and neither publication nor critical praise may define the motivating substance of our ambition. Our terms for creation, our artistic goals exist indissoluble from the living conditions and the political objectives of those whom we hope to serve well. We are the poets of our people . . . A Distinctively Black Poem will consciously seek to qualify as an instrument of survival for the poet, for her people (pp. 1 and 20).

WORKS CONSULTED

Benhabib, Seyla and Drucilla Cornell, eds.
    1987   *Feminism as Critique. On the Politics of Gender*. Minneapolis: University of Minnesota Press.

Bernal, Martin
    1987   *Black Athena. The Afroasiatic Roots of Classical Civilization*, Vol 1. New Brunswick: Rutgers University Press.

Cannon, Katie Geneva
    1985   "The Emergence of Black Feminist Consciousness," pp. 30-40 in *Feminist Interpretation of the Bible*. Ed. Letty M. Russell. Philadelphia: Westminster Press.

de Lauretis, Teresa, ed.
    1986   *Feminist Studies/Critical Studies*. Bloomington: University of Indiana Press.

Gates, Henry Louis, ed.
    1986   *"Race", Writing and Difference*. Chicago: University of Chicago Press.

JanMohamed, Abdul and David Lloyyd, eds.
    1987   *The Nature and Context of Minority Discourse*. Special Issue. *Cultural Critique*. Number 6/7.

Jordan, June
    1987   "Strong Beyond All Definition . . ," *The Women's Review of Books* 4: July-August.

Newton, Judith and Deborah Rosenfelt, eds.
    1985   *Feminist Criticism and Social Change. Sex, Class and Race in Literature and Culture*. New York: Methuen.

Petersen, Norman R.
    1985   *Rediscovering Paul: Philemon and the Sociology of Paul's Narrative World*. Philadelphia: Fortress Press.

Pryse, Marjorie and Hortense J. Spillers, eds.
    1985   *Conjuring. Black Women, Fiction, and Literary Tradition*. Bloomington: Indiana University Press.

Said, Edward W.
    1978   *Orientalism*. New York: Random House.

Schüssler Fiorenza, Elisabeth
    1983   *In Memory of Her. A Feminist Theological Reconstruction of Christian Origins*. New York: Crossroad.
    1984   *Bread Not Stone. The Challenge of Feminist Biblical Interpretation*. Boston: Beacon Press.
    1988   "The Ethics of Biblical Interpretation. Decentering Biblical Scholarship." *JBL* 107:3-17.

Snowden, Frank M., Jr.
    1979   *Blacks in Antiquity: Ethiopians in the Greco-Roman Experience*. Cambridge: Harvard University Press.

Weedon, Chris
    1987   *Feminist Practice and Poststructuralist Theory*. Oxford: Basil Blackwell.

West, Cornell
    1988   *Prophetic Fragments*. Grand Rapids: Eerdmans and Africa World Press.

Yuge, Tori and Masaoki Doi
    1988   *Forms of Control and Subordination in Antiquity*. Leiden: E.J. Brill.

SLAVE IDEOLOGY AND BIBLICAL INTERPRETATION

Katie Geneva Cannon
Episcopal Divinity School

ABSTRACT

The purpose of this paper is to unravel the various threads of ideological hegemony that lie behind the legacy of slavery in the Christian Church community, in terms of analyzing the political-social commitments which tolerated, justified and sanctioned racial chattel slavery, in order to demonstrate the interconnectedness of ideology and hermeneutics. I explore three basic myths of white Christian apologists and comment on how their oppressive practices influenced the dominant hermeneutical principle of the times. As the slave apologists thought and lived, so did the hermeneutical principle take shape.

INTRODUCTION

Scholars of stature within mainline Christian denominations have produced immense literature on the Bible and slavery with very little unanimity. Some have written about the various types of anti-slavery arguments found in the Old and New Testaments. Others have engaged in rigorous historico-critical exegesis of selected Scriptures used to condone slavery. What is interesting in the recent analyses by liberationists is the direct correlation between apologetic selectivity and the exegetes' political-social commitments. Thus, my particular concern as a liberation ethicist is to unmask the hermeneutical distortions of white Christians, North and South, who lived quite comfortably with the institution of chattel slavery for the better part of 150 years. Slaveholders knew that in order to keep racial slavery viable that in addition to legal, economic and political mechanisms they needed religious legitimation within the white society.

Apostles of slavery kept their eyes on the economic benefits and power relations at all times. Beneath their rhetoric and logic, the question of using the Bible to justify the subordination of Black people was fraught with their desire to maintain their dominance, to guarantee their continued social control. If the powerbrokers of the antebellum society were to continue benefitting from the privileges and opportunities the political economy provided, then the slaveholding aristocrats must, as a basic precondition, maintain their domination over the ideological sectors of society: religion, culture, education and media (Gramsci: 5-23; West: 9-127). The control of material, physical production required the control of the means of mental, symbolic production as well.

The practice of slaveholding was, therefore, largely unquestioned. The majority of white Christians engaged in a passive acceptance of the giveness of the main feature of slavocracy. Any questioning of the system or identification of contradictions to social practices within Christianity was undermined by the substratum of values and perceptions justified theologically by biblical hermeneutics determined from above. The rank and file of white church membership accepted the prevailing racist ideology; identifying with the slaveholders and copying their rationales, rituals and values. They regarded slave ideology and Christian life as inseparable; they were integral parts of the same system. The defense of one appeared to require the defense of the other.

Admittedly, there were a few antislavery women and men in the mainline churches prior to the aggressive abolitionist movement of the 1830s, but as a whole the white church evaded responsibility and surrendered its prerogatives to slavocracy. For most of the years that chattel slavery existed, the mainline Protestant churches never legislated against slavery, seldom disciplined slaveholders, and at most gently apologized for the "peculiar institution."

Drawing principally upon socio-ethical sources of the late-eighteenth- and early-nineteenth century, I investigate three intellectual, hierarchal constructs that lie at the center of the Christian antebellum society. 1) At what point and under what conditions did Americans of African descent lose their status as members of the moral universe? 2) What are the ethical grounds that make the formula for "heathen conversion" intrinsically wrong? and 3) What are the hermeneutical distortions that shaped the slavocracy's polemical patterns of biblical propaganda?

The Mythology of Black Inferiority

The first ideological myth legitimizing the hermeneutical assumption of Christian slave apologists was the charge that Black people were not members of the human race. Most church governing-boards, denominational missionary societies, local churches, and clergy held the position that human beings by nature were free and endowed with natural rights. Their basic concept of human relationships was equality of all people in the sight of God. No one was superior to another, none inferior. Black people had not forfeited their freedom nor relinquished their rights. This espoused oneness of humanity clashed directly with the perception that Black people must necessarily be possessed of low nature (Jordan: 3-98; Gossett: 3-31).

To justify their enslavement, Black people had to be completely stripped of every privilege of humanity (H. Smith: 23-207). Their dignity and value as human beings born with natural rights had to be denied. Black Americans were divested so far as possible of all intellectual, cultural and moral attributes. They had no socially recognized personhood. The institution of chattel slavery and its corollary, white supremacy and racial bigotry, excluded Black people from every normal human consideration. The humanity of Black people had to be denied, or the evil of the slave system would be evident.

In other words, hereditary slavery was irreconcilable with doctrines of inalienable rights (Morgan: 5-29; Degler: 49-66). So as not to contradict their avowed principles, legislatures enacted laws designating Black people as property and as less than human (Davis: 391-421). Black people were assigned a fixed place as an inferior species of humanity. The intellectual legacy of slavocracy was the development of certain white preconceptions about the irredeemable nature of Black women and Black men as "beings of an inferior order," a sub-par species between animal and human. One of the many characterizations proposed was that Black people were irremediably different from whites, as much as swine from dogs, "they are Baboons on two legs gifted with speech" (Harris: 67).

Central to the whole hermeneutical approach was a rationalized biblical doctrine positing the innate and permanent inferiority of Blacks in the metonymical curse of Ham (Washington: 231-320). The Ham story in Genesis 9:25-27 was not only used to legitimize slavery in general, but it was also used by proslavery, prowhite supremacists to justify the enslavement of Blacks in particular. Ham became widely identified as the progenitor of the Black race and the story of the curse which Noah pronounced against Canaan, the son of his son Ham, was symbolically linked to the institution of racial slavery. In a book entitled *Bible Defense of Slavery* Josiah Priest took the position that the enslaving of Black people by the white race was a judicial act of God.

> "The servitude of the race to Ham, to the latest era of mankind, is necessary to the veracity of God Himself, as by it is fulfilled one of the oldest of the decrees of the Scriptures, namely that of Noah, which placed the race as servants under other races" (393).

Christians caught in the obsessive duality of understanding Black people as property rather than as persons concurred with both faulty exegesis and social pressure that depicted people with Black skin as demonic, unholy, infectious progenitors of sin, full of animality and matriarchal proclivities.

During the early part of the eighteenth century, state laws adopted the principle of *partus sequitur ventrem*--the child follows the condition of the mother regardless of the race of the father. Absolving all paternal responsibilities, this principle institutionalized and sanctioned sexual prerogatives of "stock breeding" with Black men and the rape of Black women by white men. What this means is that the Black woman's life was estimated in terms of money, property and capital assets. She was a commodity to be bought and sold, traded for money, land or other objects. Her monetary value was precisely calculated by her capacity to produce goods and services, combined with her capacity to reproduce "a herd of subhuman labor units" (Davis: 3-29). Hence, the Black woman as the carrier of the hereditary legal status, extended the status of slave to her children and her children's children, supposedly to the infinity of time. An entire race was condemned by the laws of a purportedly Christian people to perpetual, hereditary, unrequited servitude (Cox: 353-391; Jordan: 321-325).

The white antebellum church did not see the gross injustice of slavery. Outspoken supporters of slavery generally admitted that enslaved Blacks were mere property, a type of domesticated animal to serve as the white man's tool like any other beast of burden (Ross:11-68). And as slaveholders, white Christian citizens must have the security that neither their property nor their privilege to own people as property would be taken from them. The church made every effort by admonition and legislation to see that the authority of slaveholders was not compromised. For them, the great truth written in law and God's decree was that subordination was the normal condition of African people and their descendants (Jenkins: 90-92).

Ideas and practices which favored equal rights of all people were classified as invalid and sinful because they conflicted with the divinely ordained structure which posited inequality between whites and

Blacks. The doctrine of biblical infallibility reinforced and was reinforced by the need for social legitimization of slavery. Thus, racial slavery was accepted as the necessary fulfillment of the curse of Ham. This had the effect of placing the truthfulness of God's self-revelation on the same level of Black slavery and white supremacy (Bradley: 100-105). The institutional framework that required Black men, women and children to be treated as chattel, as possessions rather than as human beings, was understood as being consistent with the spirit, genius and precepts of the Christian faith.

The Mythologizing of Enslavement

The second ideological process that legitimated Christian slave apology was a reconstruction of history and divine action in it. It was claimed that God sent slavers to the wilds of Africa, a so-called depraved, savage, heathen world, so as to free Africans of ignorance, superstition, and corruption (Noble). It is more than passing significance that the proslavery writing portrayed Africa as the scene of unmitigated cannibalism, fetish worship and licentiousness. Using gross caricatures, slave apologists mounted an ideological offensive in justification of the ravishing of the entire continent of Africa (Rodney: 7-30). They argued that Africans by nature were framed and designed for subjection and obedience. Their preoccupation was that people designated by nature as "bestial savages" and "heathens" were destined by providence for slavery (Scherer: 29-81).

Embracing false dogma of inherent African inferiority, beneficiaries of white supremacy approximated African character as the most depraved humanity imaginable. Africans were depicted as the epitome of heathenism, "wild, naked . . . man-eating savages," and "the great ethnological clown." White Christians had to be enabled to consider it an unspeakable privilege for Africans to be brought to the Americas as slaves (Davis, 1966: 165-196). Repeatedly, they claimed that slavery saved poor, degraded and wretched African peoples from spiritual darkness.

North American Christians credited themselves with weaning Africans of savage barbarity (Washington: 103-139). Their joy in converting Africans was that they were giving to "heathens" elements of Christian civilization. Being enslaved in a Christian country was considered advantageous to Africans' physical, intellectual and moral development. Slavery exposed Africans to Christianity which made them better servants of God and better servants of men.

The popularity of "heathen conversion" was disclosed in the public reception of George Fitzhugh's *Cannibals All! or, Slaves without Masters*, who wrote that Africans, like wild horses, had to be "caught, tamed and civilized." Resting upon irrational antipathies, white Christians--prominent and common-bred alike, clearly distinguished their personhood from that of Africans. Many were convinced that African peoples were somehow irreparably inferior to and less worthy than Europeans. Fixated on the fetish of heathenism, they believed that the color of white skin proved sufficient justification to rob Africans by force and fraud of their liberty. The proper social hierarchy upon which the slave system rested--the putative inferiority of Africans and the alleged superiority of Europeans--had to remain safely intact (Washington: 1-35). Historian Winthrop Jordan declares:

> Heathenism was treated not so much as a specifically religious defect, but as one manifestation of a general refusal to measure up to proper standards, as a failure to be English or even civilized .... Being Christian was not merely a matter of subscribing to certain doctrines; it was a quality inherent in oneself and one's society. It was interconnected with all other attributes of normal and proper mer. (24).

Entirely under the power of whites, against whom they dare not to complain and whom they dare not resist, enslaved Africans were denied the right to possess property, deprived of the means of instruction, of every personal, social, civil, political and religious mode of agency. If they asserted their personhood in defiance of oppressive authority, slaveholders punished them severely.

Answerable with their bodies for all offenses, slaves were beaten with horsewhips, cowstraps and a variety of blunt weapons. They suffered scalding, burning, rape, castration, sometimes dying from such infliction. The great cruelty exhibited toward enslaved Africans resulted in instances of eyes gouged, tongues slit and limbs dismembered. The callous and brutal system of slavery required a considerable number of Africans to be marked off by brands, tattoos, wooden yokes or by iron collars with long extended spokes. The intent was to crush African people's spirit and will in order to transform an entire race of people, their lives and their labor, into basic commodities of production and reproduction. Never before U.S. chattel slavery was a people so systematically deprived of their human rights and submerged in abject misery (Patterson: 1-14).

The prevailing sentiment of American Christians–the Presbyterians, the Congregationalists, the Roman Catholics, the Quakers, the Lutherans, the Baptists, the Methodists and the Anglicans–was that African peoples deserved imperial domination and needed social control (Lincoln: 23-31). Many churches preached a gospel which declared that Black people were indebted to white Christians and bound to spend their lives in the service of whites; any provisions for food, clothes, shelter, medicine, or any other means of preservation was perceived not as legal requirement but as an act of Christian charity. This "Christian feature" of Anglo-American enslavement was interpreted as an incalculable blessing to African peoples. Africans and their descendants were much better off bound in slavery with their souls free than vice versa.

These and similar judgments bolstered the belief that Anglo-Saxons, Spaniards, Danes, Portuguese, and Dutch had a divine right to defend themselves against the intolerable suffering and absolute despotism that they imposed so heavily on others. As long as the image of Africans as "heathens" was irrevocable, then the church's attempt to Christianize via enslavement could continue indefinitely, the exploitation of Africa's natural resources could proceed without hindrance, and white Christians could persist in enjoying a position of moral superiority. Ruthlessly exploiting African people was justifiable Christian action.

Remythologizing Divine Will

The third ideological myth needed to legitimize the hermeneutical circle of Christian slave apologists was the understanding that the law of God and the law of the land gave them an extraordinary right to deprive Black people of liberty and to expose Blacks to sale in the market like any other articles of merchandise. For almost two centuries, slave apologists maintained that slavery was constantly spoken of in the Bible without any direct prohibition of it; no special law against it. And therefore, on the basis of the absence of condemnation, slavery could not be classified as sin. The presumptive evidence for many white Christians was that the absence of slaveholding from the catalogue of sins and disciplinary offenses in the Bible meant that slavery was not in violation of God's law.

Biblical scholars, along with distinguished scientists, lawyers and politicians, produced a large quantity of exegetical data denying the arbitrariness of divinely ordained slavery (How: 63-133). The foundation of the scriptural case for slavery focused on an argument that neither Jesus of Nazareth, the apostles, nor the early church objected to the ownership of slaves. The fact that slavery was one of the cornerstones of the economic system of the Greco-Roman world was stressed and the conclusion reached that for the early church the only slavery that mattered was spiritual slavery to sin, to which all were bound. Physical slavery was spiritually meaningless under the all-embracing spiritualized hope of salvation. This line of reasoning was of central importance in reconciling the masses of white Christians to the existing social order. Instead of recognizing that slavery was ameliorated by early Christianity, slave apologists used their interpretative principle to characterize slavery as a sacred institution (Peterson: 91-121).

So as to elicit white Christians' consent and approval of racial chattel slavery which, theologically, contradicted the liberation reading of the Christian gospel, some of the leading antebellum churchmen--Robert Lewis Dabney, a Presbyterian theologian, Augustine Verot, the Catholic bishop of Georgia and East Florida, and John Leadley Dagg, Baptist layman who served as president of Mercer University--presented slavery as conforming to the Divine principles revealed in the Bible. White clergy were trained to use the Bible to give credence to the legitimacy of racial chattelhood (Peterson: 12-26; 38-84). In other words, they adopted an implacable line of reasoning that made slavery an accepted fact of everyday life, not only in the entire Near East but also within normative Biblical ethical teaching. Needless to say, the New Testament instruction that slaves should be obedient to their masters was interpreted as unqualified support for the modern institution of chattel slavery. The slave system was simply a part of the cosmos (Gurowski: 165-171).

Slave apologists such as George Fitzhugh, Thomas R. Dew and William A. Smith used a hermeneutical principle that functioned so as to conceal and misrepresent the real conflicts of slave ideology and Christian life. Smith, as president of Randolph Macon College in Virginia was quite candid:

> "Slavery, *per se*, is right . . . The great abstract principle of slavery is right, because it is a fundamental principle of the social state: and domestic slavery, as an *institution*, is fully justified by the condition and circumstances (essential and relative) of the African race in this country, and therefore equally right (quoted in W. Smith, 1964:25).

Fitzhugh, a well-known essayist, and Dew, a prominent lawyer, concluded that since slavery was part of a natural order and hence in accord with the will of God, it could not be morally wrong.

Christian commentators, working largely to the advantage of wealthy aristocrats, used biblical and philosophical arguments to present slaveholders' interests and claims in the best possible light (Peterson: 17-34). For example, scholars such as How, Ross and Priest constructed "biblical facts" that permitted them to claim that the eradication of chattel slavery was inapplicable to Christian living. By using selective appeals to customary practices, they disseminated moral teachings so as to reinforce what counted as good Christian conduct. Clergy were condemned for preaching against slavery because abolition sermons were considered to be a part of a traitorous and diabolical scheme that would eventually lead to the denial of biblical authority, the unfolding of rationalism, deistic philanthropism, pantheism, atheism, socialism, or a Jacobinism akin to communism. Members of churches were warned against subscribing to antislavery books, pamphlets, and newspapers. The church condoned mob violence against anyone with abolitionist tendencies, which in turn, reassured that the existing social order would go unchallenged.

Having no desire to divorce themselves from the institution of slavery, Church governing-boards and agencies issued denominational pronouncements on behalf of the official platitudes of slave ideology. Denominational assemblies reinforced publically their compliance with the assumed principle of human chattelhood. Black people were classified as moveable property, devoid of the minimum human rights society conferred to others.

The vast majority of white clergy and laity alike, appropriated this ideology to convince themselves that the human beings whom they violated or whose well-being they did not protect were unworthy of anything better. White Christians seemed to have been imbued with the permissive view that the enslavement of Black people was not too great a price to pay for a stable, viable labor system (Conrad and Meyer: 95-130; Woodman: 303-325). In a political economy built on labor-intensive agriculture, slave labor seemed wholly "natural". The security and prosperity of slavocracy evidently enabled white Christians, slaveholders and non-slaveholders alike, to feel secure with the fruits of the system.

Through a close analysis of slave ideology and biblical interpretation we can discern the many ways that chattel slavery maintained itself even after it was any longer the most economically profitable method of utilizing natural and technological resources. The majority of white Christians had learned so well not to accept the equal coexistence of whites and Blacks in the same society (Brooks: 45). They believed that giving Black people civil parity with the white population would threaten the ease and luxury of white happiness, and perhaps dissolve the Union. For the sake of the public welfare, people with ancestors born in Europe, and not in Africa, needed to be relieved of degrading menial labor so that they could be free to pursue the highest cultural attainment. Slavery, sanctioned not just by civil law but also by natural law as well, was considered the best foundation for a strong economy and for a superior society.

Concluding Ethical Reflections

In this paper I have sketched three mythologizing processes that served as the foundational underpinnings for slave ideology in relation to white Christian life. I believe that it is important for us to trace the origin and expansion of these myths because the same general schemes of oppression and patterns of enslavement remain prevalent today and because the biblical hermeneutics of oppressive praxis is far from being dead among contemporary exegetes. As life-affirming moral agents we have a responsibility to study the ideological hegemony of the past so that we do not remain doomed to the recurring cyclical patterns of hermeneutical distortions in the present--i.e. violence against women, condemnation of homosexuality, spiritualizing scripture to justify capitalism.

My analysis shows that slave apologists worked within an interpretative framework that represented the whole transcript of racial chattel slavery as ordained by God. They systematically blocked and refuted any discourse that presented contrary viewpoints. Using theo-ethical language, concepts and categories white superordinates pressed their claims of the supposedly inherent inferiority of Black people by appealing to the normative ethical system expressed by the dominant slaveholders. The political and economic context incorporated a structure of discourse wherein the Bible was authoritatively interpreted so as to support the existing patterns of exploitation of Black people.

Antebellum Christians, abiding by the developing racial and cultural conceptions, resisted any threat to slavocracy or any challenge to the peace and permanency of the order of their own denomination. They conformed their ethics to the boundaries of slave management. It became their Christian duty to rule over African people who had been stricken from the human race and reclassified as sub-human species.

Not surprisingly, denominations sprang officially to the defense of slave-trading, slaveholding and the Christianization of Africans with ingenious economic arguments. Wealthy slaveholders transmuted a portion of their disproportionate economic profit into modes of social control by public gestures that passed as generous voluntary acts of charity. They used revenue from slave labor to pay pastors, maintain church properties, support seminaries, and sustain overseas missionaries. Seduced by privilege and profit, white Christians of all economic strata were made, in effect, coconspirators in the victimization of Black people. In other words, slave apologists were successful in convincing at least five generations of white citizens that slavery, an essential and

Constitutionally protected institution, was consistent with the impulse of Christian charity.

WORKS CONSULTED

Allen, Don Cameron
    1949   *The Legend of Noah: Renaissance Rationalism in Art, Science, and Letters.* Urbana, Ill: University of Illinois Press.

Barnes, Albert
    1855   *An Inquiry into the Scriptural Views of Slavery.* Philadelphia: Parry and McMillan.

Bell, Derrick
    1987   *And We Are Not Saved: The Elusive Quest for Racial Justice.* New York: Basic Books.

Bradley, L.R.
    1971   "The Curse of Canaan and the American Negro (Gen. 9:25-27)," *Concordia Theological Monthly* 42:100-110.

Brookes, Iveson L.
    1850   *A Defense of the South Against the Reproaches of the North: in which Slavery is Shown to Be an Institution of God Intended to Form the Basis of the Best Social State and the Only Safeguard to the Permanence of a Republican Government.* Hamburg, South Carolina: The Republican Office.

Conrad, Alfred and John Meyer
    1958   "The Economics of Slavery in the Antebellum South." *Journal of Political Economy* 66:95-130, 442-3.

Cox, Oliver C.
    1948   *Caste, Class, & Race: A Study in Social Dynamics.* New York: Doubleday.

Curtin, Philip D.
    1964   *The Image of Africa: British Ideas and Action, 1780-1850.* Madison: University of Wisconsin Press.

Davis, Angela Y.
    1981   *Women, Race & Class.* New York: Random House.

Degler, Carl N.
1959   "Slavery and the Genesis of American Race Prejudice." *Comparative Studies in Society and History* 2:49-66.

Fitzhugh, George
1857   *Cannibals All! or, Slaves without Masters*. Ed. C. Van Woodward. Cambridge: Belknap Press of Harvard University, 1960.

Frederickson, George
1971   *The Black Image in the White Mind: The Debate on Afro-American Character and Destiny, 1817-1914*. New York: Oxford University Press.

George, Carol V.R.
1973   *Segregated Sabbaths*. New York: Oxford University Press.

Gossett, Thomas F.
1963   *Race: The History of an Idea in America*. Dallas: Southern Methodist University Press.

Gramsci, Antoni
1971   *Selections from the Prison Notebooks*. Ed. and trans. Quinten Hoare and Geoffrey Norwell Smith. London: Lawrence & Wishart.

Gurowski, Adam
1860   *Slavery in History*. New York: A.B. Burdick.

Harris, J. William
1985   *Plain Folk and Gentry in a Slave Society*. Middletown, Connecticut: Wesleyan University Press.

Harrison, Beverly W.
1985   *Making the Connections: Essays in Feminist Social Ethics*. Boston: Beacon.

Haselden, Kyle
1959   *The Racial Problem in Christian Perspective*. New York: Harper Torch Books.

Hosmer, William
1853   *Slavery and the Church*. Auburn, New York: William J. Moses.

How, Samuel Blanchard
    1856   *Slaveholding Not Sinful, The Punishment of Man's Sin, Its Remedy, The Gospel of Jesus Christ.* New Brunswick, New Jersey: J. Terhune's Press.

Jenkins, William Sumner
    1935   *Pro-Slavery Thought in the Old South.* Chapel Hill: University of North Carolina Press.

Jordan, Winthrop D.
    1969   *White Over Black: American Attitudes Toward the Negro, 1550-1812.* Baltimore: Penguin Books.

Lincoln, C. Eric
    1984   *Race, Religion and the Continuing American Dilemma.* New York: Hill and Wang.

Lynd, Staughton, ed.
    1967   *Class Conflict, Slavery and the United States Constitution: Ten Essays.* Indianapolis: Bobbs-Merrill.

Marable, Manning
    1983   *How Capitalism Underdeveloped Black America.* Boston: South End.

Mathews, Donald G.
    1977   *Religion in the Old South.* Chicago: University of Chicago Press.

Morgan, E.S.
    1972   "Slavery and Freedom: The American Paradox." *Journal of American History*, 59:5-29.

Noble, Frederick Perry
    1899   *The Redemption of Africa.* Chicago: Fleming H. Revell.

Okoye, Felix N.
    1971   *The American Image of Africa: Myth and Reality.* Buffalo, NY: Black Academy Press.

Patterson, Orlando
    1982   *Slavery and Social Death: A Comparative Study.* Cambridge: Harvard University Press.

Peterson, Thomas Virgil
    1978   *Ham and Japheth: The Mythic World of Whites in the Antebellum South.* Metuchen, New Jersey: The Scarecrow Press.

Priest, Josiah
 1843 *Slavery, As It Relates to the Negro, or African Race, Examined in the Light of Circumstances, History and the Holy Scriptures; with an Account of the Origin of the Black Man's Color, Causes of His State of Servitude and Traces of His Character as Well in Ancient and Modern Times.* Albany, New York: C. Van Benthuysen & Co.

Reimers, David M.
 1965 *White Protestantism and the Negro.* New York: Oxford University Press.

Rodney, Walter
 1972 *How Europe Undeveloped Africa.* London: Bogle l'Ouverture.

Rose, Willie Lee, ed.
 1976 *A Documentary History of Slavery in North America.* New York: Oxford University Press.

Ross, Frederick A.
 1857 *Slavery Ordained of God.* Philadelphia: J.B. Lippincott.

Ruchames, Louis
 1969 *Racial Thought in America: From the Puritans to Abraham Lincoln.* Amherst: University of Massachusetts Press.

Scherer, Lester B.
 1975 *Slavery and the Churches in Early America 1619-1819.* Grand Rapids, Michigan: Wm. B. Eerdmans.

Schüssler Fiorenza, Elisabeth
 1983 *In Memory of Her: A Feminist Theological Reconstruction of Christian Origins.* New York: Crossroad.

Scott, James C.
 1985 *Weapons of the Weak.* New Haven: Yale University Press.

Smith, H. Shelton
 1972 *In His Image, But . . . Racism in Southern Religion, 1780-1910.* Durham, North Carolina: Duke University Press.

Smith, William A.
 1856 *Lectures on the Philosophy and Practice of Slavery, as Exhibited in the Institution of Domestic Slavery in the United States: With the Duties of Masters and Slaves.* Nashville: Stevenson & Evans.

Washington, Joseph R., Jr.
 1984 *Anti-Blackness in English Religion, 1500-1800.* New York: Edwin Mellen.

Weatherford, W.D.
 1957 *American Churches and the Negro.* North Quincy, MA: Christopher.

West, Cornel
 1982 *Prophesy Deliverance! An Afro-American Revolutionary Christianity.* Philadelphia: Westminster.

Woodman, Harold
 1963 "The Profitability of Slavery: A Historical Perennial." *Journal of Southern History* 29:303-25.

DISCOVERING THE BIBLE IN THE NON-BIBLICAL WORLD

Kwok Pui Lan
Chinese University of Hong Kong, Hong Kong

Abstract

For many centuries, the Bible has been brought into interaction with the "non-biblical" world. It has often been taken as a norm to judge other cultures and seldom do people, biblical scholars included, feel the need to re-discover the Bible through the issues raised by people whose lives and cultures are not shaped by the biblical vision.

This paper attempts to discuss biblical interpretation in the context of the politics of truth, addressing the issue of how the Bible has been used as a tool of domination. It then discusses how Asian Christians have re-interpreted the Bible through the creative act of dialogical imagination. Finally, it presents my own understanding of the Bible from a Chinese woman's perspective.

"To the African, God speaks as if He (sic) were an African; to the Chinese, God speaks as if He (sic) were a Chinese. To all men and women, the Word goes out over against their particular existing environment and their several cultural settings." Thus spoke T.C. Chao, a Protestant theologian from China (1947:482). The central *Problematik* of biblical hermeneutics for Christians living in the "non-Christian" world is how to hear God speaking in a different voice--one other than Hebrew, Greek, German or English.

Christianity has been brought into interaction with Chinese culture for many centuries, but the Christian population in China never exceeded one percent. Since the nineteenth century, the Christian missionary enterprise has often been criticized as being intricately linked to western domination and cultural imperialism. Chinese Christians have been struggling with the question of how to interpret the biblical message to our fellow Chinese, the majority of whom do not share our belief.

In fact, this should not only be a serious concern to the Chinese, but a challenge to all Christians with a global awareness, and to biblical scholars in particular. For two-thirds of our world is made up of non-

Christians and most of these peoples are under the yoke of exploitation by the privileged one-third of our world. The interpretation of the Bible is not just a religious matter within the Christian community, but a matter with significant political implications for other peoples as well. The Bible can be used as an instrument of domination, but it can also be interpreted to work for our liberation.

This paper attempts to discuss some of the crucial issues raised by the interaction of the Bible with the non-biblical world. My observation will be chiefly based on the Chinese situation, with which I am most familiar, drawing also upon insights from other Asian theologians. I shall first discuss biblical interpretation in the context of the political economy of truth. The second part will focus on biblical interpretation as dialogical imagination based on contemporary reappropriation of the Bible by Asian Christians. Finally, I shall offer my own understanding of the Bible from a Chinese woman's perspective.

Biblical Interpretation and The Politics of Truth

Biblical interpretation is never simply a religious matter, for the processes of formation, canonization and transmission of the Bible have been imbued with the issues of authority and power. The French philosopher, Michel Foucault helps us to see the complex relationship of truth to power by studying the power mechanisms which govern the production and the repression of truth. He calls this the "political economy" of truth:

> Each society has its regime of truth, its "general politics" of truth: that is, the types of discourse which it accepts and makes function as true; the mechanisms and instances which enable one to distinguish true and false statements, the means by which each is sanctioned; the techniques and procedures accorded value in the acquisition of truth; the status of those who are charged with saying what counts as true. (131)

Foucault's analysis leads me to examine the power dynamics underlying such questions as: What is truth? Who owns it? Who has the authority to interpret it? This is particularly illuminating when we try to investigate how the Bible is used in a cross-cultural setting.

Who owns the truth? In the heyday of the missionary movement of the late 19th century, John R. Mott, the chief engineer of what was called the campaign of the "evangelization of the world in this generation" cried out:

> The need of the non-Christian world is indescribably great. Hundreds of millions are today living in ignorance and darkness, steeped in idolatry, superstition, degradation and corruption.... The Scriptures clearly teach that if men are to be saved they must be saved through Christ. He alone can deliver them from the power of sin and its penalty. His death made salvation possible. The Word of God sets forth the conditions of salvation. (17, 18)

Mott and others saw the Bible as the revealed Word of God which had to be made known to all "heathens" who were living in idolatry and superstition. The Bible was to be the "signifier" of a basic deficiency in the "heathen" culture. This is a western construction superimposed on other cultures, to show that western culture is the norm and it is superior. It might be compared to the function of the "phallus" as a signifier of the fundamental lack of female superimposed on women by men in the male psychological discourse (Lacan: 74-85). It is not mere coincidence that missionary literatures describe Christian mission as "aggressive work" (Graves: 339), and western expansion as "intrusion" (Pitcher: 47) and "penetration" (Kraemer, 1956: Table of Contents 4).

The introduction of the Bible into Asia has been marked by difficulty and resistance mainly because Asian countries have their own religious and cultural systems. The issue of communicating the "Christian message in a Non-Christian World" was the primary concern of the World Missionary Conference in 1938. Hendrik Kraemer, the key figure in the Conference, acknowledged that non-Christian religions are more than a set of speculative ideas, but are "all-inclusive systems and theories of life, rooted in a religious basis, and therefore at the same time embrace a system of culture and civilization and a definite structure of society and state" (1956: 102). But his biblical realism, influenced much by Karl Barth's theology, maintains that the Christian Gospel is the special revelation of God, which implies a discontinuity with all cultures and judges all religions (Kraemer, 1939).

This narrow interpretation of truth has disturbed many Christians coming from other cultural contexts. T. C. Chao, for example, presented a paper on "Revelation" which stated: "There has been no time, in other words, when God has not been breaking into our human world; nor is there a place where men have been that He (sic) has not entered and ruled." (1939: 42). Citing the long line of sages, moral teachers of China, such as Confucius, Mencius and Moti, he questioned, "Who can say that these sages have not been truly inspired by the spirit of our God, the God of our Lord Jesus Christ? Who can judge that the

Almighty has not appeared to them in His (sic) Holy, loving essence and that they have not been among the pure heart of whom Jesus speaks?" (1939: 43).

In this battle for truth, many Chinese Christians reject the assumption that the Bible contains all the truth and that the biblical canon is rigidly closed. Po Ch'en Kuang argued in 1927 that many Chinese classics, such as Analects, Mencius, the Book of Songs and Rites are comparable to the prophets, the Psalms, and the Book of Deuteronomy of the Old Testament (240-244). Since the Bible contains the important classics of the Jewish people which preceded Jesus, he could see no reason why the Chinese would not include their own. Others such as Hsieh Fu Ya (39-40) and Hu Tsan Yün (67-71) argue that the Chinese Bible should consist of parts of the Hebrew Bible, the Christian Bible, Confucian classics, and even Taoist and Buddhist texts! For a long time, Chinese Christians have been saying that western people do not own the truth simply because they bring the Bible to us, for truth is found in other cultures and religions as well.

Who interprets the truth? Another important issue in the political economy of truth concerns who has the power to interpret it. In the great century of missionary expansion, many missionaries acted as though they alone knew what the Bible meant, believing they were closer to truth. The Gospel message was invariably interpreted as being the personal salvation of the soul from human sinfulness. This interpretation reflects an understanding of human nature and destiny steeped in western dualistic thinking. Other cultures, having a different linguistic system and thought form may not share similar concerns. As Y.T. Wu, a Chinese theologian, notes, "Such terms as original sin, atonement, salvation, the Trinity, the Godhead, the incarnation, may have rich meanings for those who understand their origins and implications, but they are just so much superstition and speculation for the average Chinese" (836).

More importantly, this simplistic version of the Gospel functions to alienate the Christians in the Third World from the struggle against material poverty and other oppressions in their society. But in the name of a "universal gospel," this thin-sliced biblical understanding was pre-packaged and shipped all over the world. The basic problem of the so-called "universal Gospel" is that it not only claims to provide the answer but defines the question too! The American historian, William R. Hutchison (174) rightly observes that: American missionary ideologies at the turn of the century shared the belief that "Christianity as it existed in the West had a 'right' not only to conquer the world, but to define reality for the peoples of the world." If other people can only define truth according to the western perspective, then Christianization really means westernization! Chinese Christians began a conscious effort to re-define what the Gospel meant for them in the 1920's, as a response to the anti-Christian movement which criticized Christianity as "the running dog of imperialism." Chinese Christians became collectively aware that they had to be accountable to their fellow Chinese in their biblical interpretations, not just to the tiny Christian minority. They tried to show that biblical concepts such as "agape" were compatible to "benevolence" in Chinese classics and that the moral teachings of Jesus were comparable to the teachings of the Confucian tradition. As foreign invasion became imminent, the central concern of all Chinese was national salvation and the gospel message, too, became politicized (Ng: 178-179). Y.T. Wu (837), for example, reinterpreted Jesus as "a revolutionary, the upholder of justice and the challenger of the rights of the oppressed" in the mid-1930's, anticipating the kind of liberation theology that developed decades later. These attempts of indigenization clearly show that biblical truth cannot be pre-packaged, but that it must be found in the actual interaction between text and context in the concrete historical situation.

What constitutes truth? The last point I want to consider briefly concerns the norm by which we judge something as truth. Here again, Chinese philosophical tradition is very different from the west in that it is not primarily interested in metaphysical and epistemological questions. On the contrary, it is more concerned with the moral and ethical visions of a good society. The Neo-Confucian tradition in particular has emphasized the integral relationship between knowing and doing. Truth is not merely something to be grasped cognitively, but to be practiced and acted out in the self-cultivation of moral beings.

For most Chinese, the truth claim of the Bible cannot be based on its being the supposed revealed Word of God, for ninety-nine percent of the people do not believe in this faith statement. They can only judge the meaningfulness of the biblical tradition by looking at how it is acted out in the Christian community. Some of the burning questions of Chinese students at the time of foreign encroachment were: "Can Christianity save China?", "Why does not God restrain the stronger nations from oppressing the weaker ones?", "Why are the Christian nations of the west so aggressive and cruel?" (Wu: 836). These probing questions can be compared to what Katie G. Cannon, an Afro-American ethicist has also asked: "Where was the Church and the Christian believers when Black women and Black men, Black boys and Black girls, were being raped, sexually abused, lynched, assassinated, castrated and physically oppressed? What kind of Christianity allowed white Christians to deny basic human rights and simple dignity to Blacks, these same rights which had been given to others without question?" (9).

The politics of truth is not fought on the epistemological level. People in the Third World are not interested in whether or not the Bible contains some metaphysical or revelational truth. The authority of the Bible can no more hide behind the unchallenged belief that it is the Word of God, nor by an appeal to a church tradition which has been defined by white, male, clerical power. The poor, women, and other marginalized people are asking whether the Bible can be of help in the global struggle for liberation.

Biblical Interpretation as Dialogical Imagination

To interpret the Bible for a world historically not shaped by the biblical vision, there is need to conjure up a new image for the process of biblical interpretation itself. I have coined the term "dialogical imagination" based on my observation of what Asian theologians are doing. I will explain what this term means and illustrate it with some examples of the contemporary use of the Bible in Asia.

Dialogue in Chinese means talking with each other. It implies mutuality, active listening, and openness to what the other has to say. Asian Christians are heirs to both the Biblical story and to our own story as Asian people, and we are concerned to bring the two in dialogue with one another. Kosuke Koyama, a Japanese theologian, has tried to explain this metaphorically in the title of his latest book, *Mount Fuji and Mount Sinai*. He affirms the need to do theology in the context of a dialogue between Mount Fuji and Mount Sinai, between Asian spirituality and biblical spirituality (7-8). Biblical interpretation in Asia, too, must create a two-way traffic between our own tradition and that of the Bible.

There is, however, another level of dialogue we are engaged in because of our multi-religious cultural setting. Our fellow Asians who have other faiths must not be considered our missiological objects, but as dialogical partners in our ongoing search for truth. This can only be done when each one of us takes seriously the Asian reality, the suffering and aspirations of the Asian people, so that we can share our religious insights to build a better society.

Biblical interpretation in Asia must involve a powerful act of imagination. Sharon Parks (117) shows that the process of imagination involved the following stages: a consciousness of conflict (something as not fitting), a pause, the finding of a new image, the repatterning of reality, and interpretation. Asian Christians have recognised the dissonance between the kind of biblical interpretation we inherited and the

Asian reality we are facing. We have to find new images for our reality and to make new connections between the Bible and our lives.

The act of imagination involves a dialectical process. On the one hand, we have to imagine how the biblical tradition which was formulated in another time and culture can address our burning questions today. On the other hand, based on our present circumstances, we have to re-imagine what the biblical world was like, thus opening up new horizons hitherto hidden from us. Especially since the Bible was written from an androcentric perspective, we women have to imagine ourselves as if we were the audience of the biblical message at that time. As Susan Brooks Thistlethwaite suggested, we have to critically judge both the text and the experience underlying it (98).

I have coined the term "dialogical imagination" to describe the process of creative hermeneutics in Asia. It attempts to capture the complexities, the multi-dimensional linkages, the different levels of meaning in our present task of relating the Bible to Asia. It is dialogical, for it involves a constant conversation between different religious and cultural traditions. It is highly imaginative, for it looks at both the Bible and our Asian reality anew, challenging the established "order of things." The German word for imagination is *Einbildungskraft*, which means the power of shaping into one (Parks, 113). Dialogical imagination attempts to bridge the gap of time and space, to create new horizons, and to connect the disparate elements of our lives in a meaningful whole.

I shall illustrate the meaning of dialogical imagination by discussing how Asian theologians have combined the insights of biblical themes with Asian resources. We can discern two trends in this process today. The first is the use of Asian myths, legends and stories in biblical reflection. The second is the use of the social biography of the people as a hermeneutical key to understand both our reality and the message of the Bible.

For some years now, C.S. Song, a theologian from Taiwan, has urged his Asian colleagues to stretch their theological minds and to use Asian resources to understand the depths of Asian humanity and God's action in the world. He says: "Resources in Asia for doing theology are unlimited. What is limited is our theological imagination. Powerful is the voice crying out of the abyss of the Asian heart, but powerless is the power of our theological imaging" (1986: 16). To be able to touch the Hindu heart, Buddhist heart, the Confucian heart, we have to strengthen the power of theological imaging.

C.S. Song demonstrates what this means in his book, *The Tears of Lady Meng* (1981), which was originally delivered in an Assembly of the Christian Conference of Asia. Song uses a well-known legend from China, the story of Lady Meng, weaving it together with the biblical themes of Jesus's death and resurrection. In one of his recent books, *Tell Us Our Names*, Song shows how fairy tales, folk stories and legends, shared from generation to generation among the common people have the power to illuminate many biblical stories and other theological motifs. Song reminds us that Jesus was a master storyteller who transformed common stories into parables concerning God's Kingdom and human life (1984: Preface x).

The use of Asian resources has stimulated many exciting and creative ways of re-reading the scriptures. A biblical scholar from Thailand, Maen Pongudom, uses the creation folktales of the Northern Thai to contrast with the creation story in Genesis, arguing that people of other faiths and traditions share certain essential ideas of creation found in the biblical story (227). Archie Lee, an Old Testament scholar from Hong Kong, uses the role of the remonstrator in the Chinese tradition to interpret the parable of Nathan in the context of political theology in Hong Kong. His creative re-reading of the stories from two traditions shows that "story has the unlimited power to capture our imagination and invite the readers to exert their own feeling and intention" (254).

Asian women theologians are discovering the liberating elements of the Asian traditions as powerful resources to re-image the biblical story. Padma Gallup reinterprets the image of God in Genesis 1:27-28 in terms of the popular Arthanareesvara image in the Hindu tradition which is an expression of male/female deity. She argues that "if the Godhead created humans in its image, then the Godhead must be a male/female, side-by-side, non-dualistic whole" (22). I myself have used Asian poems, a lullaby, and a letter of women prisoners to interpret the meaning of suffering and hope (1984); I have also used the story of the boat people in Southeast Asia to reappropriate the theme of the diaspora (1986).

In her observations concerning the growing use of Asian resources in theologizing, Nantawan Boonprasat Lewis, a Thai woman theologian, makes the following perceptive remarks:

> The use of one's cultural and religious tradition indicates the respect and pride of one's heritage which is the root of one's being to be authentic enough to draw as a source for theologizing. On the other hand, it demonstrates a determination of hope for possibilities beyond one's faith tradition, possibilities which can overcome barriers of human expression, including language, vision, and imagination. (21)

The dialogical imagination operates not only in using the cultural and religious traditions of Asia, but also in the radical appropriation of our own history. We begin to view the history of our people with utmost seriousness in order to discern the signs of the time and of God's redeeming action in that history. We have tried to define the historical reality in our own terms and we find it filled with theological insights.

In Korean Minjung theology, Korean history is reinterpreted from the minjung perspective. Minjung is a Korean word which means the mass of people, or the mass who were subjugated or being ruled. Minjung is a very dynamic concept: it can refer to women who are politically dominated by men, or to an ethnic group ruled by another group, or to a race when it is ruled by another powerful race (Kim, 1981: 186). The history of the minjung was often neglected in traditional historical writing. They were treated as either docile or as mere spectators of the rise and fall of kingdoms and dynasties. Minjung theology, however, reclaims minjung as protagonists in the historical drama, for they are the subject of history.

Korean theologians stress the need for understanding the corporate spirit--the consciousness and the aspirations of the minjung--through their social biography. According to Kim Yong Bock: "The social biography is not merely social or cultural history: it is political in the sense that it is comprehensively related to the reality of power and to the "polis," namely the community . . . Social biography functions to integrate and interrelate the dimensions and components of the people's social and cultural experiences, especially in terms of the dramatic scenario of the people as the historical protagonists" (1985: 224).

The social biography of the minjung has helped Korean Christians to discover the meaning of the Bible in a new way. Cyris H.S. Moon (1985) reinterprets the Hebrew Bible story through the social biography of the minjung in Korea. He demonstrates how the story of the Korean people, for example, the constant threat of big surrounding nations, and the loss of national identity under Japanese colonialization, can help to amplify our understanding of the Old Testament. On the other hand, he also shows how the social biography of the Hebrew people has illuminated the meaning of the Korean minjung story. Through powerful theological imagination, Moon has brought the two social biographies into dialogue with one another.

The hermeneutical framework of the minjung's social biography also helps us to see in a new way the relationship between Jesus and the minjung. According to Ahn Byung Mu, the minjung are the *ochlos* rather than the *laos*. In Jesus's time, they were the ones who gathered around Jesus--the so-called sinners and outcasts of society. They might not have been the direct followers of Jesus and were differentiated from the disciples. They were the people who were opposed to the rulers in Jerusalem (138-9). Concerning the question of how Jesus is related to these minjung, theologian Suk Nam Dong says, in a radical voice, "[T]he subject matter of minjung theology is not Jesus but minjung. Jesus is the means for understanding the minjung correctly, rather than the concept of "minjung" being the instrument for understanding Jesus" (160). For him, "Jesus was truly *a part of* the minjung, not just *for* the minjung. Therefore, Jesus was the personification of the minjung and their symbol" (159).

Social biography can also be used to characterize the hopes and aspirations of the women, as Lee Sung Hee (1986) has demonstrated. The question of whether Jesus can be taken as a symbol for the women among the minjung has yet to be fully clarified. Social biography is a promising hermeneutical tool because it reads history from the underside, and therefore invites us to read the Bible from the underside as well. Korean minjung theology represents one imaginative attempt to bring the social biography of minjung in Korea into dialogue with the minjung of Israel and the minjung in the world of Jesus. It shows how dialogical imagination operates in the attempt to reclaim the minjung as the center of both our Asian reality and the biblical drama.

Liberating the Bible: Many Voices and Many Truths

After this brief survey of the history of the politics of truth in the Chinese Christian community and a discussion of dialogical imagination as a new image for biblical reflection, I would like to briefly discuss my own understanding of the Bible. I shall focus on three issues: 1) the sacrality of the text, 2) the issue of canon and 3) the norm of interpretation.

Sacrality of the text. The authority of the Bible derives from the claim that it is the Scripture, a written text of the Word of God. However, it must be recognised that the notion of "scripture" is culturally conditioned and cannot be found in some other religious and cultural traditions, such as Hinduism and Confucianism. This may partly account for the relative fluidity of these traditions, which can often assimilate other visions and traditions. These traditions also do not have a crusading spirit to convert the whole world.

Why has the Bible, seen as sacred text, shaped western consciousness for so long? Jacques Derrida's deconstruction theory, particularly his criticism of the "transcendent presence" in the text and the logocentrism of the whole western metaphysical tradition offers important insights. In an earlier volume of *Semeia* which focuses on "Derrida and Biblical Studies," the editor Robert Detweiler summarizes Derrida's challenge to biblical scholarship:

> The main characteristic of sacred texts has been their evocation and recollection of sacred presence--to the extent that the texts themselves, the very figures of writing, are said to be imbued with that divine immanence. But Derrida argues that such a notion of presence in writing is based on the false assumption of a prior and more unmediated presence in the spoken word; this spoken word in the religious context is taken to be none other than the utterance of deity, which utterance is then reduced to holy inscription in and as the text. For Derrida, however, written language is not derivative in this sense; it does not find its legitimacy as a sign of a "greater" presence, and the sacred text is not rendered sacred as an embodiment of an absolute presence but rather as the interplay of language signs to designate "sacred". (1982:1)

The notion of the "presence" of God speaking through the text drives us to discover what the "one voice" is, and logocentrism leads us to posit some ultimate truth or absolute meaning which is the foundation of all other meanings. But once we recognise the Bible is one system of language to designate the "sacred," we should be able to see that the whole biblical text represents one form of human construction to talk about God. Other systems of language, for example, the hieroglyphic Chinese which is so different from the Indo-European languages, might have a radically different way to present the "sacred." Moreover, once we liberate ourselves from viewing the biblical text as sacred, we can then feel free to test and reappropriate it in other contexts. We will see more clearly the meaning of the text is very closely related to the context and we will expect a multiplicity of interpretations of the Bible, as Jonathan Culler says, "meaning is context-bound but context is boundless" (128).

The issue of Canon. Canonization is the historical process which designates some texts as sacred and thus authoritative or binding for the religious community. This whole process must be analysed in the contest of religio-political struggles for power. For example, scholars have pointed out that the formation of the canon of the Hebrew Bible was imbued with the power-play between the prophets and priests. The New Testament canon was formed in the struggle for "orthodoxy" against such heresies as Marcionism and Gnosticism. Recently, feminist scholarship has also shown how the Biblical canon has excluded Goddess worship in the Ancient Near East and that the New Testament canon was slowly taking shape in the process of the growing patriarchalization of the early church.

The formation of the canon is clearly a matter of power. As Robert Detweiler so aptly puts it: "A Text becomes sacred when a segment of the community is able to establish it as such in order to gain control and set order over the whole community" (1985: 217). This was true both inside the religious group as well as outside of it. Inside the religious community, women, the marginalized and the poor (in other words, the minjung), did not have the power to decide what would be the truth for them. Later, when Christianity was brought to other cultures, the biblical canon was considered to be closed, excluding all other cultural manifestations.

As a woman from a non-biblical culture, I have found the notion of canon doubly problematic. As my fellow Chinese theologians have long argued, Chinese Christians cannot simply accept a canon which relegates their great cultural teachings and traditions to the secondary. As a woman, I share much of what Carol Christ has said, "women's experiences have not shaped the spoken language of cultural myths and sacred stories" (1979: 230). Women need to tell our own stories, which give meaning to our experience. As Christ continues, "We must seek, discover, and create the symbols, metaphors, and plots of our own experience" (1979: 231).

I have begun to question whether the concept "canon" is still useful, for what claims to safeguard truth on the one hand can also lead to the repression of truth on the other. A closed canon excludes the many voices of the minjung and freezes our imagination. It is not surprising that feminist scholars of religion are involved in the rediscovery of alternate truths or the formulation of new ones. Rosemary R. Ruether's recent book (1985b), *Womanguides* is a selection of readings from both historical sources and modern reformulations that are liberating for women. Elisabeth Schüssler Fiorenza's reconstruction of the early Christian origins (1983) borrows insights from non-canonical sources. Carol Christ (1980) describes women's spiritual experiences from women's stories and novels. Black women scholars such as Katie G. Cannon (1985) and Delores Williams (1985) have also emphasized black women's literature as resources for doing theology and ethics. These stories of the liberation of women as well as other stories from different cultural contexts must be regarded as "sacred" as the biblical stories. There is always the element of holiness in the people's struggle for humanhood, and their stories are authenticated by their own lives and not the divine voice of God.

The Norm for Interpretation. Since I reject both the sacrality of the text and the canon as a guarantee of truth, I also do not think that the Bible provides the norm for interpretation in itself. For a long time, such "mystified" doctrine has taken away the power from women, the poor and the powerless, for it helps to sustain the notion that the "divine presence" is located somewhere else and not in ourselves. Today, we must claim back the power to look at the Bible with our own eyes and to stress that divine immanence is within us, not in something sealed off and handed down from almost two thousand years ago.

Because I do not believe that the Bible is to be taken as a norm for itself, I also reject that we can find one critical principle in the Bible to provide an Archimedian point for interpretation. Rosemary Ruether has argued that the "biblical critical principle is that of the prophetic-messianic tradition," which seems to her to "constitute the distinctive expression of biblical faith" (1985a: 117). This is highly problematic for three reasons: 1) The richness of the Bible cannot be boiled down to one critical principle. Ruether often makes comments like "God speaks through the prophet or prophetess . . . . the spokesperson of God . . . ." (1985a: 117), as if the utterance of God is the guarantee of the one principle. Here again we discern the need for "absoluteness" and "oneness" which Derrida questions. The minjung need many voices, not one critical principle. 2) The attempt to find something "distinctive" in the Biblical tradition may have dangerous implications that it is again held up against other traditions. 3) Her suggestion that this critical principle of the Bible can be correlated with women's experiences assumes that the prophetic principle can be lifted from the original context and transplanted elsewhere. She fails to see that the method of correlation as proposed by Tillich and Tracy presupposes the Christian answer to all human situations, an assumption which needs to be critically challenged in the light of the Third World situation today.

Conversely, I support Elisabeth Schüssler Fiorenza's suggestion that a feminist interpretation of the Bible must "sort through particular biblical texts and test out in a process of critical analysis and evaluation how much their content and function perpetuates and legitimates patriarchal structures, not only in their original historical contexts but also in our contemporary situation" (1985: 131). The critical principle lies not in the Bible itself, but in the community of women and men who read the Bible and who through their dialogical imagination, appropriate it for their own liberation.

The communities of minjung differ from each other. There is no one norm for interpretation that can be applied cross-culturally. Different communities raise critical questions to the Bible and find diverse segments of it as addressing their situations. Our dialogical imagination has infinite potential to generate more truths, opening up hidden corners we have failed to see. While each community of minjung must work out their own critical norm for interpretation, it is important that we hold ourselves accountable to each other. Our truth claims must be tested in public discourse, in constant dialogue with other communities. Good news for the Christians might be bad news for the Buddhists or Confucianists.

The Bible offers us insights for our survival. Historically, it has not just been used as a tool for oppression, because the minjung themselves have also appropriated it for their liberation. It represents one story of the slaves' struggle for justice in Egypt, the fight for survival of refugees in Babylon, the continual struggles of anxious prophets, sinners, prostitutes and tax-collectors. Today, many women's communities and Christian base communities in the Third World are claiming the power of this heritage for their liberation. These groups, which used to be peripheral in the Christian Church, are revitalizing the Church at the center. It is the commitment of these people which justifies the biblical story to be heard and shared in our dialogue to search for a collective new religious imagination.

In the end, we must liberate ourselves from a hierarchical model of truth which assumes there is one truth above many. This biased belief leads to the coercion of others into sameness, oneness, and homogeneity which excludes multiplicity and plurality. Instead, I suggest a dialogical model for truth each has a part to share and to contribute to the whole. In the so-called "non-Christian" world, we tell our sisters and brothers the biblical story that gives us inspiration for hope and liberation. But it must be told as an open invitation: what treasures have you to share?

(I am grateful to Kesaya Noda for editing the manuscript and to the Asian Women Theologians, U.S. Group, for mutual support and challenge.)

WORKS CONSULTED

Ahn, Byung Mu
    1981   "Jesus and the Minjung in the Gospel of Mark." Pp. 136-51 in *Minjung Theology: People as the Subjects of History*. Ed. Kim Yong Bock. Singapore: The Commission on Theological Concerns, Christian Conference of Asia.

Chao, T.C.
    1939   "Revelation." Pp. 22-57 in *The Authority of the Faith*. New York: International Missionary Council.
    1947   "The Articulate Word and the Problem of Communication." *IRM* 36:482-89.

Cannon, Katie Geneva
"A Theological Analysis of Imperialistic Christianity."
(Unpublished paper)
1985 "Resources for a Constructive Ethic in the Life and Work of Zora Neale Hurston." *JFSR* 1: 37-51.

Christ, Carol P.
1979 "Spiritual Quest and Women's Experience." Pp. 228-45 in *Womanspirit Rising: A Feminist Reader in Religion*. Ed. Carol P. Christ and Judith Plaskow. San Francisco: Harper & Row.
1980 *Diving Deep and Surfacing: Women's Writers on Spiritual Quest*. Boston: Beacon.

Culler, Jonathan
1982 *On Deconstruction: Theory and Criticism After Structuralism*. Ithaca, New York: Cornell University Press.

Detweiler, Robert
1982 "Introduction." *Semeia* 23: 1-2.
1985 "What is a Sacred Text?" *Semeia* 31: 213-30.

Foucault, Michel
1980 *Power/Knowledge: Selected Interviews and Other Writings, 1972-1977*. Ed. Colin Gordon. New York: Pantheon.

Gallup, Padma
1983 "Doing Theology--An Asian Feminist Perspective." *Commission on Theological Concerns Bulletin, Christian Conference in Asia* 4: 21-27.

Graves, R.H.
1877 "How Shall the Native Church be Stimulated to More Aggressive Christian Work." Pp. 338-46 in *Records of the General Conference of the Protestant Missionaries of China held at Shanghai, May 10-24, 1877*. Shanghai, China: Presbyterian Mission Press.

Hsieh Fu Ya
1974 "Kuan-hu chung-hua chi-tu-chiao sheng-ching ti pien-ting wen-t'i" (On the issues of editing the Chinese Christian Bible). Pp. 39-40 in *Chung-hua chi-tu-chiao shen-hsueh lun-chi* (Chinese Christian Theology Anthology). Hong Kong: Chinese Christians Book Giving Society.

Hu Tsan Yün
1974 "Liang-pu chiu-yüeh" (Two Old Testaments). Pp. 67-71 in *Chung-hua chi-tu-chiao shen-hsueh lun-chi*. Hong Kong: Chinese Christians Book Giving Society.

Hutchison, William R.
1982 "A Moral Equivalent for Imperialism: Americans and the Promotion of Christian Civilization, 1880-1910." Pp. 167-78 in *Missionary Ideologies in the Imperialist Era: 1880-1920*. Ed. Torben Christensen and William R. Hutchison. Aros.

Kim, Yong Bock, ed.
1981 *Minjung Theology: People as The Subjects of History*. Singapore: The Commission on Theological Concerns, Christian Conference of Asia.
1985 "Minjung Social Biography and Theology." *Ching Feng* 284:221-31.

Koyama, Kosuke
1984 *Mount Fuji and Mount Sinai: A Critique of Idols*. Maryknoll, New York: Orbis.

Kraemer, Hendrik
1939 "Continuity or Discontinuity." Pp. 1-21 in *The Authority of The Faith*. New York: International Missionary Council.
1956 *The Christian Message in a Non-Christian World*, 3rd ed. Grand Rapids, Michigan: Kregel.

Kwok, Pui Lan
1984 "God Weeps with Our Pain." *East Asian Journal of Theology*, 22: 228-32.
1986 "A Chinese Perspective." Pp. 78-83 in *Theology by the People: Reflections on Doing Theology in Community*. Ed. Samuel Amirtham and John S. Pobee. Geneva: World Council of Churches.

Lacan, Jacques and the école freuidienne
1982 *Feminine Sexuality*. Ed. Juliet Mitchell and Jacqueline Rose. Trans. Jacqueline Rose. New York: W.W. Norton.

Lee, Sung Hee
1986 "Women's Liberation Theology as the Foundation for Asian Theology." *East Asia Journal of Theology*, 42: 2-13.

Lee, Archie C.C.
    1985   "Doing Theology in the Chinese Context: The David-Bathsheba Story and the Parable of Nathan." *East Asia Journal of Theology* 32: 243-57.

Lewis, Nantanwan Boonprasat
    1986   "Asian Women's Theology: A Historical and Theological Analysis." *East Asia Journal of Theology*, 42:18-22.

Moon, Cyris H.S.
    1985   *A Korean Minjung Theology: An Old Testament Perspective*. Maryknoll, New York: Orbis/Plough.

Mott, John R.
    1972   *The Evangelization of the World in This Generation*. New York: Arno. (Reprinted from the Original 1900 Edition).

Ng Lee Ming
    1978-79   "The Promise and Limitation of Chinese Protestant Theologians, 1920-50." *Ching Feng*, 214-22:175-82.

Parks, Sharon
    1986   *The Critical Years: The Young Adult Search for a Faith to Live By*. San Francisco: Harper & Row.

Pitcher, P.W.
    1893   *A History of the Amoy Mission, China*. New York: Board of Publication of the Reformed Church in America.

Po Ch'en Kuang
    1927   "Chung-kuo ti chiu-yüeh" (Chinese Old Testament). *Chen-li yu sheng-ming* (Truth and Life) 2: 240-44.

Pongudom, Maen
    1985   "Creation of Man: Theological Reflections based on Northern Thai Folktales." *East Asia Journal of Theology* 32: 222-27.

Ruether, Rosemary Radford
    1985a   "Feminist Interpretation: A Method of Correlation." Pp. 111-24 in *Feminist Interpretation of the Bible*. Ed. Letty M. Russell. Philadelphia: Westminster.
    1985b   *Womanguides: Readings Toward a Feminist Theology*. Boston: Beacon.

Schüssler Fiorenza, Elisabeth
    1983   *In Memory of Her: A Feminist Theological Reconstruction of Christian Origins*. New York: Crossroad.

	1985	"The Will to Choose or to Reject: Continuing Our Critical Work." Pp. 125-36 in *Feminist Interpretation of the Bible.* Ed. Letty M. Russell. Philadelphia: Westminster.

Song, C.S.
  1981   *The Tears of Lady Meng.* Geneva: World Council of Churches.
  1984   *Tell Us Our Names: Story Theology from an Asian Perspective.* Maryknoll, New York: Orbis.
  1986   *Theology from the Womb of Asia.* Maryknoll, New York: Orbis.

Suk, Nam Dong
  1981   "Historical References for a Theology of Minjung." Pp. 155-84 in *Minjung Theology: People as the Subjects of History.* Ed. Kim Yong Bock. Singapore: The Commission on Theological Concerns, Christian Conference of Asia.

Thistlethwaite, Susan Brooks
  1985   "Every Two Minutes: Battered Women and Feminist Interpretation." Pp. 96-107 in *Feminist Interpretation of the Bible.* Ed. Letty M. Russell. Philadelphia: Westminster.

Williams, Delores
  1985   "Black Women's Literature and the Task of Feminist Theology." Pp. 88-110 in *Immaculate & Powerful: The Female in Sacred Image and Social Reality.* Ed. Clarissa W. Atkinson, Constance H. Buchanan and Margaret R. Miles. Boston: Beacon.

Wu, Y.T.
  1937   "The Orient Reconsiders Christianity." *CC* 54: 835-38.

HISTORICAL/CULTURAL CRITICISM AS LIBERATION: A PROPOSAL FOR AN AFRICAN AMERICAN BIBLICAL HERMENEUTIC

Vincent L. Wimbush
School of Theology, Claremont

Abstract

Historical and cultural criticism can serve to aid minority, culturalist readings of the Bible to stand with integrity against alien imperialistic readings. Historical criticism is necessary in order to gain perspective on the historically determined nature of all religious constructs, including those in biblical texts. Cross-cultural analysis is necessary in order to interpret the symbols and referents of biblical cultures and contemporary dominant cultures, so as to determine which symbols and referents from any culture are relevant and affirming.

I. Introduction

Not all solutions or agenda are good for everyone; nor are all "good" solutions "good" for everyone at the same time. Every people must respect and assess its own immediate social, political and economic situation, its own problems and challenges, and apply the needed remedies in light of the assessed situation; to do less or otherwise can be self-defeating, perhaps, even pathological and genocidal. What may have been good strategy in Birmingham or Selma can be disastrous in Johannesburg or Managua.

This principle of self-assessment and self-remedy, of "Know thyself" and "Heal thyself," is no less relevant in the sphere of things religious; it could hardly be different, since religious matters are not apolitical, asocial, or unaffected by history. So not even all "liberation" theologies, or hermeneutical constructs are liberating for all peoples. Since different peoples have different histories and experiences, and find themselves in different social, political and religious situations, not all prescriptions for salvation *should* be respected by all peoples.

With regard to the interpretation of the Bible as part of a religious liberation agenda, every "reading" is, and must always be recognized as, *culture-specific*. Thus, even every potentially "liberating" hermeneutical construct must reflect the *history* of that people to be liberated.

The traditional historical-critical methods have been viewed by some as inadequate for, even detrimental to, efforts to construct a liberation-oriented hermeneutic. Those for whom the methods are inadequate--including biblical scholars!--often employ the methods, but see the necessity of going beyond them in the attempt to construct "liberation" theologies (Schüssler Fiorenza; Gottwald; Schottroff/Stegemann for some representative names of scholars). And, of course, there are those--among them some theologians, activist clerics and laypersons--who not only see no relevance for liberation struggles in the methods, but are convinced of their obfuscating powers on those who utilize them. The methods, after all, were developed and are employed by those who must be cast among modern day oppressors.

But this "solution," like all others, must be assessed in light of specific situations and histories. The question of *origins* is of minor importance--in isolation from concern about *function*. The question about the relevance or potential power of critical methods in the study of the Bible in any religious liberation strategy must be addressed ultimately in terms of a people's history, and how such methods could service that people in its present situation.

My reading of the African-American past and present situation leads me to advocate the necessity of the historical-critical and cultural-critical study of the Bible among African-Americans both for their survival and as an aid in their quest for liberation in the fullest possible sense of the word. What is first required in support of this position is at least an historical outline of the religious experiences of African-Americans in order to gain perspective for commentary on the present religious situation facing African Americans.

II. Historical Outline:
From Physical to Hermeneutical Bondage

The experience of being uprooted from their homeland, enslaved and placed in a strange and hostile environment, must be considered the *presupposition* of African-Americans' religious experience and heritage (Long). The African slave in North America was at first without a language with which communication with slavers and, to some extent, other slaves, could be realized. But this state of affairs did not obtain for long. The Africans did find a language, indeed, a language world through which they began to wax eloquent not only with the slavers, not only among themselves, but also about themselves, about the ways in which they understood themselves in the strange new world. The language, indeed, language world was that of the Bible.

That the Bible has played an important role in the history of African Americans nearly all comprehensive interpreters at least acknowledge, even if they do not attempt to explain. The Africans in the North American colonies could not fail to notice the powerful presence and influence of the Bible upon the Europeans' self-image. Among their first reactions to the Europeans was a combination of wariness, suspicion, hostility and awe with respect to the Bible--a book--as the Europeans' sacred object (Raboteau: 242). The point that the white slaveholding developing nation was conceptually wrapping itself in the "Holy Book," defining itself by "the Book," acknowledging its source of power (including imperialistic and racist hegemony) in "the Book," was not lost on the Africans. It did not take the Africans long to associate "Book Religion" with power, with survival (Turner: 271-88; Gill: 226-28).

Since their initial engagement with the Bible African-Americans have always sought to articulate their self-understandings, their problems and challenges and aspirations through biblical rhetoric and imagery. All African American leaders--clerical and non-clerical--have for the most part functioned as *biblical theologians* for their people. But very few of these leaders have had as their primary frame of reference the academic study of the Bible, with its historical and critical concerns (Wimbush: 9-11).

In the period--nineteenth century--of the introduction of the use of critical methods in the study of the Bible in North America, African Americans had already begun to appropriate Christian symbols, concepts and language, viz., the Bible, in their own way. This appropriation, and their collective social status in American society, made irrelevant for them the crises that led to the adoption of the critical methods in the study of the Bible, and resulted from the adoption of the methods in the study of the Bible. The African American "reading" of the Bible did not fit neatly into the doctrinalist, moralist, or pietist readings of the Bible with which the various communions of the dominant society can be associated (Mouw:139-62; Fogarty:163-80). Since the vast majority of African Americans, from the beginning of their experience in the Americas, were denied opportunity to learn to read and write, the "letters" of the biblical texts were not crucial in their appropriation of Christian traditions. What became important in African American *Christian* origins was the *telling* and *re-telling*, the *hearing* and *re-hearing* of biblical stories--stories of difficult sojourn, of perseverance, of faith, of survival, or ultimate victory (Matthews:212-36; Mays:19-96; Raboteau:239f). Identification with the heroes and heroines of the Bible, with the "people of God," with the persecuted, suffering, but ultimately victorious Jesus constituted "faith." Obviously, this engagement of the Bible as the single most important depository of Christian tradition was directly influenced and determined by African Americans' political, economic and social *experience*.

This experience-based African religion ultimately inspired the independent African church movements (Graveley:59-68). The independent churches were founded to enable African Americans to survive (Wilmore:220-41) with meaning the dehumanizing forces of the dominant society (including its religions), as well as "uplift the race" in every facet of life.

But these churches soon found themselves in a theological dilemma which would prove to have ramifications far beyond the church walls. Although the churches were founded in response to the social situation in which African Americans found themselves, most of the leadership in the churches nevertheless assumed continued adherence to the confessional frameworks (creeds, liturgies and polities) of the dominant society to be innocent. Afro-Baptists continued to respect Anabaptist and/or Calvinist statements of faith; African Methodists continued to hold the line for Wesleyan doctrine and piety, as well as Episcopal polity. Both communities allowed the Euro-American theological constructs and polities to stay in place while they explained their existence on an altogether different basis (Paris:42-52).

But, of course, dogma, liturgies and polities are not innocent; they serve important social functions, including the enhancing of solidarity and influencing of personal and communal behavior (Malina, 1986a). No confessional framework should ever be embraced with innocence, that is, without attention to the implications for social self-understanding and social orientation in the world.

But the uncritical embrace of alien confessional frameworks which has characterized African American religious experience in the past now begins to have the most deleterious effects upon African Americans. No longer can they either innocently or uncritically embrace the confessional frameworks of other peoples without having to face enormous problems--social, political, economic. The worlds of the late eighteenth century, the nineteenth century and, perhaps, even the early twentieth century afforded African Americans the physical and conceptual space--on account of the legacy of slavery, disenfranchisement, and segregation--in which to *relativize* all the structures of American society, including religious structures. Thus, it was then possible for African Americans to embrace religious/confessional frameworks rather innocently.

But no more! Pseudo-integrationism in churches, neighborhoods, schools (including seminaries!) in American society, the power of the media and jet travel to force upon us a bland homogeneity--these and other factors have made embrace of alien confessional frameworks anything but innocent and, potentially, self-destructive and pathological. Now it is precisely because it can be claimed at least that an American is an American is an American, or that fundamentalism "'must rest on the Word,' be unified in theology, not culture, color, or history . . . ." (*Christianity Today*:44) that African Americans must be discerning.

Without discernment already fundamentalism has been able to attract a significant number of African Americans. Not unlike the precipitants which led to the rise of fundamentalism in the dominant society in the early decades of the twentieth century, the rise of fundamentalism among African Americans can be understood as a response to a crisis of enormous proportions, a crisis of thinking, of security. White Protestant America at the end of the nineteenth century and in the first decades of the twentieth century was faced with the onslaught of change in every area of life--the scientific revolution, a world war, new weapons, new scientific methods and questions. The changes were collectively so great that they effectively represented and forced a "paradigm shift" of consciousness (Weber:101-20). Nothing would remain the same, although some, concerned with "fundamentals," with the old paradigm, would attempt to deny change.

African Americans were not a significant part of the beginnings of the fundamentalist movement in the United States (Marsden:228). Only in recent decades have African Americans come to embrace it. The embrace seems to reflect a rejection of racialist or culturalist religion.

It is with respect to biblical interpretation, especially, that the dilemma faced by African American churches is most clearly evident. Along with every confessional framework comes some set of presuppositions about the appropriate manner in which the Bible as Holy Scripture should be read. Different traditions are more or less perspicuous on this matter. Because of its importance in all interpretations of Christian existence, the Bible--and clarity about the way it should be engaged--should never be taken for granted as a powerful communal right and responsibility. Since all readings of the Bible are political and have political implications, no community can afford to embrace any hermeneutic uncritically.

The Bible should be the focus of the challenge that Afro-Christian churches must begin to address in order to embrace and define Christian traditions anew for affirmation and liberation. For without an increased measure of *hermeneutical control* over the Bible, it will prove impossible for Afro-Christian churches to articulate self-understanding, maintain integrity as separate communities, and determine their mission in the world. The gravity of the challenge for African American churches is deepened as it is kept in mind that no other African American institution or organization can possibly claim to be able to articulate African Americans' collective yearnings and aspirations.

Both *defense* from imperialistic hermeneutical constructs (and with them symbols, concepts, rituals, polities, and political philosophies) and *indigenous control* over their own traditions are required for African American liberation understood in its broadest sense. Basically *pre-critical* in their biblical hermeneutics, burdened by their embrace of integration as an ideal, located in a dominant society in which the boundaries of ethnic identity and traditions are ever more porous and difficult to maintain, African Americans find themselves unable sometimes even to recognize alien and non-affirming claims from other religious traditions, especially those which court with similar language and polities. They also find it difficult to build upon their own foundations, since self-criticism and constructive change in a tradition are frustrated without historical consciousness and critical disposition. A proposal for the historical-critical and cultural-critical study of the Bible is in order.

III. Biblical-Historical Study as Liberation: Self-Defense

Historical study of the Bible is required on the part of the African American churches for the sake of self-criticism and self-defense. The historically-conscious community as reader of the biblical texts would be made aware of their historically determined character. Historically conscious readings serve to make all interpreting communities--from whatever social world, with whatever set of social experiences--more honest.

There is nothing inherent in the notion of the Bible as "Holy Scripture" which should preclude any people, including African Americans, from engaging the Bible as a collection of historically conditioned documents. Descriptive, historical investigation is, in fact, all the more needed when the Bible is understood as "Holy Scripture:"

> ... the more intensive the expectation of normative guidance and the more exacting the claims for the holiness of the Scripture, the more obvious should be the need for full attention to what it meant in the time of its conception and what the intention of the authors might have been. But where the Bible is enjoyed in a far more relaxed mood as a classic, people do like to find its support or sanction for their thoughts

and actions. The low intensity of the normativeness often makes such use of Scripture less careful (Stendahl:8).

The historical study of the Bible does not assume objectivity. On the contrary, the historical and critical study assumes biases on the part of the interpreter, and often keeps them before the interpreter. Since there is always at work a "construal," "a logistically prior and imaginative decision" (Kelsey:198-99) in every tradition about how to read the Bible, historical critical study of the Bible can serve to keep before any interpreting community its own operating "construal," as well as its chronological and psychic *distance* from the world of the Bible. Such study will inevitably force the responsible interpreting community to acknowledge the *discontinuity* and the *non-repeatability* of the Bible vis-a-vis the modern world (White:112).

For African Americans much is at stake in being able to understand religious traditions, including their own, as historical movements. In the published version of the Haskell Lectures in Comparative Religion (Chicago) Kurt Rudolph argued that there are five specific areas in which the historical study of religions may yield fruit, especially for the poor and oppressed of the modern world: First, it may engage in the critique of specifically *religious* traditions. Second, the practice of critiquing religious traditions would have "an enlightening and emancipating" impact upon the self-understanding of contemporary religious communities. Third, it can pursue critically the changing relationships between religion and politics, especially with respect to issues relating to the political, social, economic dominance on the part of certain religious communities, the marginalization of others. Fourth, it can address Marx's understanding of religion as "the opium of the people," on the one hand, as "the protest against distress," on the other, as a way of coming to grips with the relationship between religion and social structure in general. Fifth, it can shed light on the religious yearnings and aspirations of the "religious underground" of the world, that such might be understood in historical terms and respected for both difference and similarities (75-76).

That the potentially liberating impact of the types of investigations outlined above for the poor and oppressed peoples of the world is not lost on Rudolph is reflected in his quoting of Karl-Otto Apel's *Transformation der Philosophie:*

> The direct, dogmatic and normative approach of the understanding of tradition, established institutionally and socially obligatory, functioned within Europe until the Enlightenment and in most cultures outside Europe up to the present time. Now, however, it can no longer be revived ... By being alienated inevitably from their own traditions, the third-world cul-

tures testify that systems of meaning--for example, religious and moral orders of value--must be conceived in closest connection with the forms and institutions of social life. Above all, they seek a philosophical and scientific orientation that mediates the hermeneutical understanding of their own and of foreign traditions of meaning through sociological analyses of the respective economic and social orders. This more than anything else makes it easy to understand the power Marxism has to fascinate intellectuals of developing countries (76).

IV. Historical/Cultural Criticism as Liberation: Towards Construction of a Hermeneutic

The important and necessary offices of the historical-critical investigation of the Bible notwithstanding, it cannot provide what is needed if African Americans are to be strong and articulate about themselves. What is required is an affirming indigenous biblical hermeneutic which would reflect African Americans' self-understanding as a people with a heritage and a future. Historical critical reading of the Bible can very effectively aid African Americans in an effort to disentangle themselves from the existential trajectories of the dominant society in the United States, in an effort to see their own unique history over against both the biblical world and the post-biblical interpreting the world around them. Such reading can help African Americans see more clearly what biblical texts may have *meant*.

But questions remain and must therefore be posed: What now for African Americans should/do the texts *mean*? To reformulate and re-direct the question Catholic biblical scholar Raymond Brown directed to fellow Catholics: would African Americans be richer in their engagement of Christian realities as a result of the use of historical-critical methods on the part of African American biblical scholars (White:112; Brown:86)?

It is not likely that the employment of the historical-critical methods alone would result in much more than the equipping of African Americans for a self-defensive posture, a "suspicious" negative hermeneutic relative to the hermeneutical constructs of other peoples and communions. The methods themselves would neither spare African Americans the biases which have afflicted other peoples and communions nor automatically provide African Americans with the cure-all hermeneutic. What must follow the necessarily distancing and dissembling and relativizing effects of the historical study of biblical texts must be an effort to re-interpret such texts for the more affirming indigenous hermeneutic as the challenge.

No re-interpretive effort, however, will prove to be worthy of consideration if it does not reflect awareness of the importance of *cross-cultural* analysis, so that the temptation to collapse biblical worlds into the contemporary world of African Americans can be avoided. Crosscultural analysis is a *sine qua non* for the construction of an indigenous hermeneutic to the extent that it can translate the meaning of "symbolic referents" from one culture to another, viz., the way in which one world "works" for another (Malina, 1986b:92). Without this "translation" the interpreter, even the historically conscious interpreter, can make the mistake of assuming that some differences and distance notwithstanding, the worlds of the Bible basically "worked" the same way, that certain concepts and terms basically meant the same thing.

The comparative study of cultures gives the interpreter a perspective from which the cultures of the Bible can be seen not only as historically different, but also fundamentally, viz., culturally different. Such perspective would force the question about the *relevance* of any discussion or prescription in biblical texts for any contemporary cultural context.

> Anyone who tries to ground a Christian ethics for contemporary Americans in the Bible has to know what a biblical norm means when Americans hear it. It is after all a matter of life and death when we consider that Paul's statement that all authority is from God played a major role in the creation of the "good German" who obeyed orders throughout the Third Reich. Paul addressed . . . communities, lacking any power to upset or further the aims of the Roman empire. Telling such people to respect the authorities as coming from God reassured the powerless that God would care for them, and served to deter rebellion that would have brought down imperial wrath on Paul's powerless communities. German Christians governed their world (White:114).

No re-integration, no re-interpretation of biblical texts can take place in any truly liberating way unless first it is established how the culture, the world of the biblical text works and is structured, and how the working of the culture of the biblical text squares with the culture of the interpreter. Obviously, this squaring can be done only if the interpreter is working with a model of interpretation which would provide a grid for comparative analysis. Only then can the interpreter, even the historically conscious interpreter, escape, as much as it is possible, culture-bias.

African Americans stand to benefit greatly from a hermeneutic which not only sees the references to slavery in the New Testament texts as things of the past (historical-critical study), but also sees them as part of the political response of a specific sub-culture of fictive kinship groups within an imperialistic empire. The slavery described by and condoned by fictive kinship groups in such a setting could hardly be the same as that slavery which was the empire's. Further, the slavery described and condoned by the fictive kinship groups of the first century Mediterranean world surely cannot be used to support the more modern day slave trafficking on the part of European and American imperialists. The latter cannot possibly be identified as *both* "brothers" and "sisters" *and* as empires.

Cultural criticism will allow no re-interpretation of biblical texts until cultural referents, symbols and meanings are translated. African Americans can profit from such investigation because no biblical text would then be deemed relevant until it is clear that the cultural referents and terms of the respective biblical worlds have meaning in their own world and can be made applicable in that world. Otherwise, they should be willing to say of a biblical text that it is not (Holy Scripture) for them.

V. Concluding Statements

That the historical/cultural critical study of the Bible--as the study not only of biblical antiquity, but of post-biblical engagements of the Bible--is potentially liberating, especially for minority communities in American society, should be clear. With America's Bible-based origins and self-understanding, with its present head of state defining himself as pontifex maximus, officially giving the Bible its own year, no minority culture can survive or defend its integrity against it without historical and cultural critical study of the bible. The capacity to sustain a minority culturalist reading of the Bible within the context of North American culture, with its powerful media, with its integrationist and conformist ideals, is most difficult without a critical framework. No people can hear God through any medium without knowing both the medium and the worlds which are being mediated.

WORKS CONSULTED

Brown, Raymond E.
    1985   *Biblical Exegesis and Church Doctrine.* New York: Paulist.

Christianity Today,
    23 May 1980.

Fogarty, Gerald P.
    1982   "The Quest for a Catholic Vernacular Bible in America." Pp. 163-80 in *The Bible in America: Essays in Cultural History.* Ed. Nathan O. Hatch and Mark O. Noll. New York: Oxford University Press.

Gill, Samuel D.
    1982   *Beyond the "Primitive": The Religions of Nonliterate Peoples.* Englewood Cliffs, New Jersey: Prentice-Hall.

Gottwald, Norman K., ed.
    1983   *The Bible and Liberation. Political and Social Hermeneutics.* Maryknoll, New York: Orbis.

Graveley, Will B.
    1984   "The Rise of African Churches in America (1786-1822): Re-examining the Contexts," *JRT* 41:58-73.

Kelsey, David H. *The Uses of Scripture in Recent Theology.* Philadelphia:
    1975   Fortress.

Long, Charles H.
    1971   "Perspectives for a Study of Afro-American Religion in the U.S." *HR* 2:54-66.

Malina, Bruce
    1986a   *Christian Origins and Cultural Anthropology: Practical Models for Biblical Interpretation.* Atlanta: John Knox.
    1986b   "'Religion' in the World of Paul." *BTB* 16:92-101.

Marsden, George M.
    1980   *Fundamentalism and American Culture: The Shaping of Twentieth Century Evangelicalism: 1870-1925.* New York: Oxford University Press.

Matthews, Donald G.
    1977   *Religion in the Old South.* Chicago: University of Chicago Press.

Mays, Benjamin E.
1969   *The Negro's God as Reflected in His Literature.* New York: Atheneum.

Mouw, Richard J.
1982   "The Bible in Twentieth Century Protestantism: A Preliminary Taxonomy." Pp. 139-62 in *The Bible in America: Essays in Cultural History.* Ed. Nathan O. Hatch and Mark O. Noll. New York: Oxford University Press.

Paris, Peter J.
1985   *The Social Teaching of the Black Churches.* Philadelphia: Fortress.

Raboteau, Albert J.
1978   *Slave Religion: The "Invisible Institution" in the Antebellum South.* New York: Oxford University Press.

Rudolph, Kurt
1985   *Historical Fundamentals and the Study of Religions.* New York: Macmillan.

Schottroff, Willy and Wolfgang Stegemann, eds.
1984   *God of the Lowly: Socio-Historical Interpretations of the Bible.* Trans. Matthew J. O'Connell. Maryknoll, New York: Orbis.
[*Der Gott der kleinen Leute: Sozialgeschichtliche Bibelauslegungen.* Vol. 1, Altes Testament and vol. 2, Neues Testament. Munich: Chr. Kaiser Verlag, and Gelnhausen/Berlin/Stein: Borckhardthaus-Laetare, 1979].

Schüssler Fiorenza, Elisabeth
1983   *In Memory of Her: A Feminist Theological Reconstruction of Christian Origins.* New York: Crossroad.

Stendahl, Krister
1984   "The Bible as a Classic and the Bible as Holy Scripture. *JBL* 103:3-10.

Turner, Harold W.
1979   *Religious Innovation in Africa: Collected Essays on New Religious Movements.* Boston: G.K. Hall.

Weber, Timothy P.
    1982   "The Two-Edged Sword: The Fundamentalist Use of the Bible." Pp. 101-20 in Hatch and Noll.

White, Leland T.
    1986   "The Bible, Theology, and Cultural Pluralism." *Biblical Theological Bulletin* 16:111-15.

Wilmore, Gayraud S.
    1983   *Black Religion and Black Radicalism: An Interpretation of the Religious History of Afro-American People.* 2d ed. rev. and enlarged. Maryknoll, New York: Orbis.

Wimbush, Vincent L.
    1986   "Biblical-Historical Study as Liberation: Toward an Afro-Christian Hermeneutic." *JRT* 42:9-21.

"MOTHER TO THE MOTHERLESS, FATHER TO THE FATHERLESS": POWER, GENDER, AND COMMUNITY IN AN AFROCENTRIC BIBLICAL TRADITION*

Cheryl Townsend Gilkes
Colby College

ABSTRACT

The Bible is an important interpretive tool by which Africans and their descendants in the United States placed their cultural experience in a religious framework and constructed an Afro-Christian tradition. Fragments of the Bible found in songs, sermons, and prayers represent important evidence of this cultural imagination. This paper examines one such biblical fragment and the manner in which the Afro-Christian tradition appropriated it. Within gospel music, the biblical phrase, "father to the fatherless" (Ps. 68:5) has been linked to such parallel phrases as "mother to the motherless," "brother to the brotherless," and "sister when you're sisterless." This usage points to the special importance of Psalm 68 for black people and extends the image of God to include the feminine and the maternal in worship language. Gender as a religio-cultural issue is linked to the problems of power, community, ethnic identity, and hope. In addition to a distinctive Afro-American cultural emphasis, this biblical tradition, as an example of the hermeneutics both of suspicion and of affirmation, contributes to the liberationist reconstruction of biblical study in the Church.

Most black Christians have heard the statement that God is both "a mother to the motherless, and a father to the fatherless." Additional variations remind them that God is a "friend to the friendless" or a "sister to the sisterless" or a "brother to the brotherless." While never heard during the "scripture reading," it was heard during the prayers, the gospel songs, or the sermons. "Everybody knew" that God was both "mother to the motherless" and "father to the fatherless." It never occurred to these black people that this combined feminine and masculine image of God could possibly be an issue. Instead they took comfort in knowing that God was there in the powerlessness and abandonment of their life situations. Thus there was hope in the worst circumstances imaginable. Along with the assurance of Psalm 27 that if their mothers or fathers forsook them that God would surely "take them up," they found the image of God as a "mother to the motherless" and a "father to the fatherless" a comforting tradition.

Houston Baker (3-4) offers "a vernacular theory" of the "distinctive culturally specific aspects of Afro-American literature and culture." Using the blues as his focus, he argues that ". . . Afro-American culture is a complex, reflective enterprise . . ." and this complexity is expressed in the blues. Such a cultural expression should be viewed as "a matrix" or ". . . a point of ceaseless input and output, a web of intersecting, crisscrossing impulses, always in productive transit." Applying Baker's model, Afro-American religious tradition is also such a matrix. Particularly, the Afro-centric biblical tradition represents another "ancestral matrix that produced a forceful and indigenous American creativity."

This paper examines this image of God as a "mother to the motherless and father to the fatherless," as an expression of the "Afrocentric idea." For Asante, the Afrocentric idea, a world view that seeks to interpret and understand, is expressed in the oral tradition of black people in worship and in the rhetoric of resistance central to that oral tradition. It emerges out of the creative matrices of the black experience and is a cultural creation. It draws upon the materials at hand to construct myth and to confront the human condition of oppression--a principal preoccupation of African-American spokespersons. The images of God in songs, sermons, prayers, and testimonies are important Afrocentric expressions in the United States. DuBois (178) called them "the imprint of Africa on Europe in America." The images "mother to the motherless and father to the fatherless" illustrate this Afrocentric use of the King James Bible as a liberating resource and creative "matrix."

An Afrocentric reading of the Bible exhibits a variety of techniques that shape a biblical tradition relevant to the black condition. One technique is the extension of or enlargement upon a passage to tailor the imagery of a text to concrete circumstances. Placing the phrase "mother to the motherless" alongside the biblical fragment "father to the fatherless," is such an example. Although God's relationship to the fatherless is a central prophetic theme, this particular phrase, "father to the fatherless," is found only in Ps. 68. The prominence of this fragment identifies Psalm 68 as an historically and politically charged reference to the black experience. The Afrocentric usage of this psalm, a discourse on divine power, points to the importance of gender. Black people imaged a God of power as both male and female although they were initially presented with a patriarchal God in an androcentric text. Why should gender elicit such a theological response? For powerless people, images of power are important. Given the patriarchal power arrangements of the historical and contemporary United States, this connection between the feminine and the powerful is important.

Psalm 68 serves as a place where African communities on the continent and in diaspora turned to insist upon their inclusion in the salvation history and future promises of the gospel. Issues of gender and power are fused in a context that blesses African identity and communal integrity and rejects the norms of a racist society, claiming a past and a future for black people. This claim to a future underscores the centrality of hope in an Afrocentric reading. Psalm 68, as used, expresses revolutionary perspectives, maintains the relevance of the Bible as an ethical resource from which Afro-Americans can shape social change, and makes a dramatic cultural statement concerning gender.

"Our God is Able": An Afrocentric Folk Text

Although the connections between God as "father of the fatherless" and "mother to the motherless" can be heard throughout the Afro-Christian tradition, the gospel song, "Surely God is Able," is largely responsible for fixing this in popular consciousness. The rise of gospel music in the late 1920's and early 1930's in the United States continued a line of cultural development, the spirituals and the blues (Walker). Hostility to the new music pushed gospel singers into secular settings such as concert halls and theaters (Heilbut). The popularity of records expanded this development. Popular songs found their way into the pulpits and prayers and covenant meetings of black churches. And traditional expressions from pulpits, prayers, and covenant meetings found their way back into the copyrighted gospel composition.

"Surely Our God Is Able" was immensely popular. It was written by Rev. Herbert Brewster, a Memphis, Tennessee minister, who collaborated with an arranger named Virginia Davis and, some believe, a singer named Isabella Jones. The song was popularized by Clara Ward and the Ward Singers. Brewster was known as a biblical composer and drew his images directly from the statement of Shadrach, Meshach, and Abednego in response to the threat of the fiery furnace: ". . . Our God whom we serve is able to deliver us from the burning fiery furnace. . . . (Daniel 3:17/KJV)". The superscription of the song quotes several verses of scripture along with Daniel 3:17: Romans 4:21 ("What he had promised he was ABLE to perform."); 2 Corinthians 9:8 ("For God is ABLE to make him stand."); and 2 Timothy 1:12 ("I am persuaded that he is ABLE to keep that which I have committed to his trust."). In his commentary, Brewster wrote, "From these bold Scriptural Declarations we give you this Gospel-Spiritual with a prayer that some souls may take fresh courage and comfort in the theme with which it deals and ever be soothed and sustained in the truth that 'GOD IS ABLE.' "

The verses of the song affirm God's power, God's care and concern for the desolate pilgrim, God's presence in difficult circumstances, and God's overall sustaining power. "As pilgrims we sometimes journey;/We often know not which way to turn;/But there is one who knows the road;/He'll help us carry our heavy load." The chorus then insists, "Don't you know God is able!.../Clouds may gather, all around you/So dark and sable." Making the connection between "our God" and "the form of the fourth is like a Son of God" (Dan 3:25, KJV), the next verse states, "He walked into the furnace door,/With Shadrach, Meshach, and Abednego; He took the heat out of the flame, I know to day, He's just the same." The third verse conflates Romans 4:21 with the incident of the Philippian jail: "One night He shook the Roman jail,/Prisoners stood free on Heaven's bail;/Yes that same God still rules the world,/His flag of truth is still unfurled." Finally the song returns to the book of Daniel, concluding, "He stepped into the lion's den/Protected Daniel who slept therein; The next day Daniel told the king,/My God is able, rescue to bring."

The song then moves into its litany of biblical-theological images, "He was Daniel's stone a-rolling;/And Ezekiel's wheel turning;/He was Moses' bush burning;/He was Solomon's Rose of Sharon;/He was Joshua's mighty battle axe./Surely, surely, Surely, surely, He's able to carry you through." After presenting these biblical images, the chorus is then repeated presenting an additional litany: "He'll be your friend when you're friendless;/He's a mother for the motherless;/He's a father for the fatherless;/He's your joy when you're in sorrow;/He's your hope for tomorrow;/When you come down to the Jordan,/He'll be there to bear your burden;/He's gonna step out before you;/In the judgment, He's got to know you./Oh, surely. . . . He's able to carry you through." Other artists include such statements as: "He's your sister, when you're sisterless;/He's your brother, when you're brotherless;/He's a doctor in the sickroom;/He's a lawyer in the courtroom."

As an Afrocentric folk text, the song points to the vitality of the Afro-Christian biblical tradition and some specific connections that black Christians made and it draws upon biblical traditions and upon the existential reality of the black community. It connects a personal God who cares about the individual's circumstances with a powerful liberating God. The song is an Afrocentric reading of the King James Bible and conveys that Afrocentric tradition in a new and highly popular way. It combines the basic affinity for the liberating dimensions of the Hebrew Bible with an insistence that images of God be affirmed in the experience of black persons and their community. The song combines several hermeneutical voices (Schüssler Fiorenza, 1984:15-18). Its voice of *suspicion* that opposes the evangelical suppression of the Hebrew Bible's communal salvation. Its voice of *remembrance* connects the God of Moses, Joshua, Daniel, and Ezekiel with contemporary suffering. The content and style of the song carry the voice of *creative actualization* by involving the listeners. With its call and response and its highly stylized affirmation ("Oh yes!, Ooh, ooh!), the song becomes a ritual drama that orchestrates the interplay of these voices. In time, the song and its traditional foundations came to be part of what "everybody knows" in the black church, that "God is a mother to the motherless and a father to the fatherless."

The King James Bible as an Afrocentric Matrix

An immediate problem for the Africans and African-Americans who adopted biblical Christianity was the appropriation of the Bible to represent their world view and address their particular situation. Unlike their owners, they read the psalms in a liberationist perspective and they connected the theophanic language of the psalter with such language in apocalyptic, historical, and prophetic texts.

Observers have pointed to the importance of the Bible in black religion (Raboteau, 1978; Sobel, 1979; Webber, 1976; Mitchell, 1977). This can be seen especially in the spirituals and in black literature (Bartel, 1975). That legacy is carried over into gospel music where sheet music notations often carry references to biblical passages. Others have noted the centrality of the Bible to the preaching tradition with its emphasis on telling the story (Johnson, 1927, Buttrick, 1987) and prayer traditions (Carter, 1976). During slavery, biblical religion encountered African survivals and the influence of the African world view. In their new situations, "Africans . . . were summarily required to relinquish their principal cultural insignia, including religion. . ." Rather than fatalistic resignation, "they could make a conscious effort at the redetermination of their destiny and their identity within the context of their developing body of Western experience" (Lincoln:62).

Sobel (1979) and Stuckey (1987) demonstrate that the process of cultural transformation was much more complex than was previously thought. Sobel reconstructs the historical process through which black people arrived at an "Afro-Baptist world view." Black people moved from their "West African sacred cosmos" through the transformations of language and intergenerational circumstances (3-21). The biblical record in black oral tradition indicates that the Bible was an important tool in this transformation. Aided by the similarities of their West

African backgrounds and the significant force of the common slave experience, Africans developed a very negative response to Anglo-American religion. Sobel (40) observes that " . . . the African had a basic disrespect for white religion. . . . Through special efforts, white ministers did win a limited number of converts, but the *Afro-Americans by and large rejected Anglicanism. Moreover, blacks "laught" at the devotions of new black Christians."* (Emphasis mine.) Changes that included participation in revivals, the revision of African spirituality, and the active choice of Baptist polity with its emphasis on liberty produced an institutional and spiritual reality that was African-American and Baptist--an "Afro-Baptist sacred cosmos" (Sobel:139-80). She concludes, "Despite internal and external pressures, the new black Baptist world view held together, uniting the African and the Baptist cosmos both perfectly and imperfectly (180)."

For any captive or oppressed group, the hermeneutical and constitutive tasks of culture take on crisis proportions. As captive people in a hostile new world, confronted with an oppressor's language, Africans needed to reconcile both African and Anglican cultural materials--a multi-faceted hermeneutical task. The constitutive and hermeneutical tasks Africans faced in building religious meanings and institutions in the United States involved African religious memory. Both the "involuntary presence of the black community in America," and "Africa as historical reality and religious image" contributed to the specifically religious elements in the religion of black Americans (Long: 172-75). For Africans and their descendents in the United States, their choice of a Baptist world view and polity meant that they were able to use the Bible as a tool in the construction and revision of meaning.

Africans who were offered the Christian tradition faced a contradiction. They were asked to share and give assent to the religion that reinforced the culture and social organization that was destroying their lives and exploiting their labor and degrading their personhood. For them to assume uncritically the revelations of their owners would have been the first step in a complex process of cultural genocide. Given the ideological importance of the Bible for racism and slavery, African-Americans needed to develop their own understanding of its meaning for their lives and their faith. Long points out that the Bible played an important role in this community that drew heavily from a folkloric tradition. "To be sure, the imagery of the Bible plays a large role in the symbolic presentations. . . . The biblical imagery was used because it was at hand; it was adapted to and invested with the experience of the slave."

Strangely enough, it was the slave who gave a religious [read biblical] meaning to the notions of freedom and land. The deliverance of the children of Israel from the Egyptians became an archetype which enabled the slave to live with promise. Since the descendants of these Africans are part of religious traditions in which the English Bible (usually King James) is a central feature, the biblical fragments and passages left behind are important matrices or meaning transformers, that enabled them to construct a distinctive and meaningful tradition. The religious foundations of any culture's future are bound up in the presentation of the past and the way that past informs the present. Using their Bibles as a matrix, they reinterpreted their past in order to cope with and look beyond their oppressive present. This Afrocentric reading of the Bible represents the way in which Africans and their descendents utilized the "Blessed Book" to speak to their past, present, and future situations.

The preaching of Sojourner Truth, not only in her famous women's rights speech but also in her other speeches and her personal theme ("Proclaim liberty throughout the land"), highlights the importance of the Bible even to those who could not read (Sterling:150-51). Maria Stewart made heavy use of the Bible in her speeches. She appealed specifically to Psalm 68 as evidence that black people were included in biblical promises (Richardson). Howard Thurman recounted his task of reading the Bible to his grandmother (a freedwoman) when he was a child. In the aftermath of slavery, learning to read the Bible was so important that "the gospel and the primer" became inseparable (Litwack:450). Freed women and men used "this Blessed Book" (Litwack:471) to defend their institutions and their individual and communal religious experiences immediately after slavery, when their distinctive style was assaulted by black and white missionaries. For David Walker and others the Bible represented an important resource for the validation of African humanity as part of the people of God.

Thus, an Afrocentric reading of the Bible is a reading that incorporates the events that are central to the black experience and affirms the dignity of the African personality in the face of the forces of degradation; such a reading rejects the use of Bible as an apology for oppression and it is quick to point out the categorical inclusion of Africans. This inclusion becomes the basis upon which the text can be expanded upon and augmented to include the range of experiences that are peculiarly African and African-American and yet affirm the universality of the good news. Through a variety of folktexts, the Afrocentric reading captures the multivalent dimensions of the oppression. Ultimately an Afrocentric reading of the Bible is an important contribution to an ever expanding hermeneutic of suspicion growing out of many theologies of liberation and to a hermeneutic of affirmation and of creative actualization that have roots in the preaching traditions of black churches.

The problems of powerlessness and injustice are central themes in the Bible. The category "fatherless" is extremely large and God as "father to the fatherless" is reinforced in the Anglican prayer tradition, something the Africans and their descendants borrowed in spite of their rejection of the worship tradition. The genius of this Afrocentric reading of the Bible is its recognition of the central issues of powerlessness, justice, and theodicy in a context where the dominant "canon within the canon" did not. Hanks (ix) described his response when he noted this omission in the dominant exegetical tradition. He reflected, "Imagine my shock when I consulted work after work of First World biblical erudition . . . and found almost nothing! My initial reaction was one of perplexity, frustration, and indignation." The Afrocentric reading discerned what Hanks (4) discovered: that "oppression. . . [is] *a basic structural category of biblical theology.*"

Biblical definitions of oppression embraced the slaves' experience. The Bible identified multiple "forms and methods of oppression." Tamez (41), summarizing this biblical perspective, writes: "The oppressors are thieves and murderers, but their ultimate purpose is not to kill or impoverish the oppressed. Their primary objective is to increase their wealth at whatever cost. The impoverishment and death of the oppressed are a secondary consequence." There are two levels of oppression: the international and the national. Black people experienced both and they observed this in their close relationship with Native peoples in the South. At the international level that oppression described in the Bible consists of "the enslavement and exploitation of . . . workers, . . . genocide, . . . [ideologies and] myths of idleness, . . . deceitful concessions, . . . [crushing violent force], . . . plunder and slaughter, . . . the imposition of tribute, . . . and exile (41-45)." Slaves knew they were exploited workers. They experienced the genocidal dimensions through the murders and tortures of slavery and the Middle Passage. They were victimized by the myths of idleness embedded in such stereotypes as Sambo (Blassingame). Story after story of slaves cheated out of their opportunity to buy their own or their family members' freedom spoke to the problem of deceitful concessions. The excessively brutal responses to slave revolts and the decades of post-bellum terror reinforced biblical images of plunder and slaughter. Even the problem of exile--the legal and customary inability to live as free persons in slave areas--was prominent in slave consciousness. Manumission could mean the loss of family and community. Women's low rates of escape reflect these constraints of family and community.

Even the "national" dimensions of biblical oppression, "exploitation of workers, . . . fraud, [and] . . . [violence] murder," were evident in the black experience. The Bible also counseled against lending systems or "usury" that perpetuated an oppressed state and southern sharecroppers of the late nineteenth and early twentieth centuries had no trouble recognizing the biblical opposition to their plight. The Bible also cited "sexual violation of women" as one of the central "methods" of oppression. The disparity of strength was so great that rape was sometimes imaged as a form of murder (Tamez:46-53).

In their reading of Psalm 68 and by extension the other psalms that speak directly of the "poor," the "fatherless," the "widow," "the weak," and the "captive," slaves understood that they were poor and in need of liberation. In recognizing their "fatherlessness" black people grappled with their "natal alienation" or "social death" (Patterson). Their humanity was legally stripped from them and their only realistic challenge was moral and religious in a society where ideologies of freedom and citizenship abounded. Psalm 68 as part of their Afrocentric reading became a promise of ultimate empowerment. As the biblical "fatherless" and therefore God's people, they were endowed with rights and privileges. Their emphasis on "Jubilee" as an aspect of liberation and freedom perceived that even in biblical slavery, a challenge existed to the injustice they experienced. The Bible offered a vision of economic equity and citizenship. Redemption or salvation incorporated economic and political empowerment and a restoration to civil status.

Slaves' view of themselves as motherless addressed the powerlessness of their family and community systems. That view recognized the devastating assault on women within the system of racial oppression. Black men wrote most of the slave narratives that account for the suffering of women, usually their mothers or other relatives. They lamented the neglect that stemmed from slave women's exploitation as nurses and caretakers of white children. They described the pervasive violence and sexual abuse in the slave system. The physical and ideological assaults on black mothers were major manifestations of cultural humiliation. The powerlessness of women to withstand sexual victimization was an emblem of group oppression.

By connecting motherlessness and fatherlessness, the Afro-Christian tradition provided a comprehensive portrait of powerlessness. It was a civil, economic, political, and cultural problem combined. Fatherlessness linked with motherlessness apprehended the particularities of the black situation. The theological perspective in the Afrocentric reading assesses the morality of oppression, particularly the morality of the oppressors themselves. Intuitively, this Afrocentric approach recognized what Tamez (53) describes as a basic characteristic of oppressors: "The oppressors are rich and influential people. . . ; their basic concern is to accumulate wealth. They . . . are idolaters who follow false gods that can lend an aura of legitimacy to their actions . . . ." Since Psalm 68 spoke of the necessity for all to turn to God, oppressors were brought under its judgment. In opposition to the oppressors' attempts to ideologize the Bible, this reading upheld the Bible's original judgment of power and oppression.

Psalm 68: A Matrix for Afrocentric Hermeneutics

Critical perspectives on Psalm 68 indicate that African Americans read it differently from Europeans. Exegetes have difficulty dating the psalm or eliciting a coherent meaning from it. Overviews that classify and type the psalms ignore Psalm 68 entirely. Regardless of the correctness or incorrectness of Afro-Americans' reading in the context of technical exegesis, it is important to note the ways in which this psalm--a real puzzle to exegetes--became a locus of meaning and group religious actualization. According to Taylor (353), "The classification of this psalm is difficult because it has no exact counterpart in the Psalter. On first impression it is a liturgical medley of songs and hymns strung along without any governing motif. . . ." While those who discuss it agree that it is difficult, its actual date and purpose vary widely among interpreters. After assessing its difficulties, Taylor argues that it is "post exilic (354)." Another critic, building on the work of W.F. Albright, describes the psalm "as textually and exegetically the most difficult and obscure of all the psalms (Dahood: 133)." He argues that it can only be understood in an extra-biblical context that compares it with other poetry from the Ancient Near East and dates it, along with Albright, in "the Solomonic period." Anderson (35) cites it, along with Psalms 18 and 29, as primary examples of "how heavily indebted Israel was to the surrounding culture, especially to the Canaanites . . . ." Gray associates the psalm with an autumn covenant renewal festival and also suggests that it was recorded in the time of Solomon and later revised for Temple worship. According to Hoppe's interpretation of Tronina's work, the psalm represents an elaboration on the wilderness wanderings in Numbers 33. Other dates place the psalm during the preaching of First Isaiah (Schildenberger), Second Isaiah (Yoffre), and, based on a comparison with Psalm 98 and other "divine warrior victory songs, either during the Exodus or during the Second Temple" (Longman). An earlier critical perspective (Briggs) sees it as a late summary of "the victories of Yahweh in the long history of Israel."

In the King James Version, the basis for the Afrocentric reading, this Psalm is a majestic song that speaks of power throughout. It begins with a statement of God's ultimate victory, "Let God arise, let his enemies be scattered." Using the metaphor of smoke and melting wax, we see the fate of those who "hate him." Because of this victorious God, the "righteous" are able to "exceedingly rejoice" and "be glad." They are commanded to "Sing unto God, sing praises to his name" in one of only two places (the other is Psalm 83:18) where the divine name ("JAH") is spelled out (Anderson:25). Verse five and six then describe this God who is named by saying, "A father of the fatherless,/and a judge of the widows,/is God in his holy habitation./God setteth the solitary in families:/he bringeth out those which are bound with chains:/but the rebellious dwell in a dry land." God is, in these few short lines, a liberator, a parent, and a bringer of justice ("judge") to those least able to care for themselves in the society.

The psalm then continues on to describe God's action in the wilderness and the dramatic response of nature to God's presence--a response to a God of power, whose chariots "are twenty thousand," and who commands "thousands of angels." This God of power then imprisons captivity and provides benefits for the people, who we have already learned in verse 10 are "the poor." God also promises deliverance even "from the depths of the sea." After these promises of deliverance and triumph, the psalm becomes a description of the praise accorded God "in the sanctuary." Not only do we find "singers" and timbrel playing "damsels," but we see the princes of the tribes of Israel and kings bringing presents. Finally (verse 30), the psalmist(s) petitions God to "rebuke" those who do not submit and sacrifice and to "scatter" those "who delight in war." Verse 31, a key verse for the Afrocentric reading states: "Princes shall come out of Egypt;/Ethiopia shall soon stretch out her hands unto God." The psalm ends with an admonition to praise this God of great power--"he that rideth upon the heavens of heavens" and whose "strength is in the clouds" and who is "terrible out of thy holy places." This strong and powerful God can be counted upon to give "strength and power unto his people."

No academic exegete would accept the King James Version as the best translation. The portions selected for emphasis reflect a people who, when reading the King James Version, identify with the people in the psalm who belong to God: "the poor," "the fatherless," "the widows," "those which are bound in chains," and "my people . . . from the depths of the sea"--those who need the gift of "strength and power." The early twentieth century (and probably late nineteenth century) view represented by Briggs (94) sees the last verses (31-35) as the product of "a later editor" who "adapts the Ps. to liturgical use by adding Messianic prediction (v. 32), invocation to public praise (vv. 33-35), and finally adoration of the God of Israel in His sanctuary (v. 36a, b)." For this critic, the section most cherished within the black tradition is not considered authentic and is, therefore, not translated in the commentary. For other critics, the references to Ethiopia or Cush were seen as examples of hostile references when taken together with reference to

Egypt and the linguistic construction that underlies the translation of vs 30, "the beast of the reed thicket (Dahood:149)." Additionally, the reference to Ethiopia, Dahood (151) states, is to that nation's wares and, when taken with Isaiah 60:1-6, the verse refers to the wealth of nations pouring into a victorious Jerusalem from vanquished enemies.

The historical critical approach to the Bible ceased to commend Psalm 68 to the Church. While the psalm is included in the Anglican lectionary and its phrase, "Father to the fatherless" occurs at least twelve times in the Anglican prayer book, it has been abandoned by other segments of the church and the newer lectionaries. Its scholarship is unclear. Exegetes cannot agree on a date for its final writing and must go outside the boundaries of Israelite experience in order to translate it. Black people used the Psalm and that use was what Sanders (1984:34) calls "community commendation." Community commendation is a step in the process of canonization whereby a community selects, repeats, and popularizes a tradition in such a way that it comes to be fixed in the canon. The believing communities of Africans in the United States selected, repeated, and popularized among themselves Psalm 68 as well as other texts that their oppressors neglected or discarded. The Afrocentric biblical tradition extended the "life" of these texts.

Afro-Americans saw themselves as objects of God's salvation at Sinai in the reference to Ethiopia or Cush. Instead of seeing a reference to the submission of one of Israel's enemies, they perceived a universal invitation to share a particular story. The universal dimensions of the psalm are found in this warrior God, who has shaken the wilderness and resided on the mountain top and whose deliverance reaches to the depths of the sea. Such a reading is beyond scholarly apprehension. Taylor (359) observed that the calls to worship and the majestic activities of God lead up to "the final exhortation of the passage: 'Let Ethiopia hasten to stretch out her hands to God.'" There is an emphasis here beyond technical translation. Taylor continues, saying, "Here in sum we have an idea of the experience of worship, coupled with the basic intention of religion, set on a very high level." While the Afrocentric reading does not conform to technical exegesis and "correct" translation, that reading does capture the spirit of "the universal recognition of Israel's God" and the understanding that "the Lord must become universally acknowledged . . . (Taylor:359)."

This arguably imprecise Afrocentric reading is important from an existential point of view. The Afro-Christian tradition has "prayed" this psalm properly (Brueggemann, 1982). The reading recognizes Afro-American kinship with the children of Israel in their moments of captivity, liberation, and worship. This Afrocentric reading is able to hear the variety of voices contained in these "human responses to God's word and actions (Westermann:10)" and it recognizes the language of liberation embedded in this psalm and throughout the Bible. The Afro-American usage engages in the "liberation of language" necessary for Christians to pray the psalms properly. Brueggemann (1982:27) emphasizes the importance of one's own experience in an encounter with the Psalms. ". . . What we bring to the Psalter in order to pray is a candid openness to the extremities in our own lives and in the lives of our fellows, extremities which recognize the depths of despair and death, which acknowledge the sheer gift of life. The work of prayer is to bring . . . together the boldness of the Psalms and the extremity of our experience . . . ."

Part of the total disregard for the humanity of oppressed peoples is a disregard for the integrity of their communities and their histories. For black people in the United States, a reclamation of their humanity and historical peoplehood was a central task of cultural construction. The importance of this task required that it be answered in a religious context. The classical challenge, "Am I not a man and a brother?" (a question extended, interestingly enough, by Maria Stewart to woman and sister) was answered repeatedly in the preaching and prayers of the black tradition. The claim of black people to be children of God was one that had to be brokered in an oppressive structure where the oppressors also claimed to be children of God. They sang affirmatively, "If anybody asks you who I am, just tell them I'm a child of God." In the slave quarters community, white religion was seen as false religion. Folklore stories of empty white heavens and desegregated heavens affirmed this.

The reference to "Ethiopia" became a promise that affirmed their humanity, ethnic identity and community. It enabled black Christians to account for the now and the not yet. On the one hand, Ethiopians were included in God's vision of salvation and their conversion and inclusion were ordained in scripture. To deny the humanity of black people and the integrity of their communities was to fly in the face of God's will and further risk God's wrath. "Ethiopia" as a present reality gave the community moral integrity and permitted resistance to an oppressive denial of humanity and solidarity with other "children of God."

The promise of Ethiopia also became a vehicle for a "dangerous memory." Not only does this dangerous memory account for suffering, exclusion, and conflict, but it is also "a memory of hope, a memory of freedom and resistance (Welch:39)." The Afrocentric folktext, as a theological interpretation of spiritual and social experience, does what liberation theology is supposed to do. Welch (41) describes liberation theology as the "preservation of dangerous memory . . . of resistance and liberation" declaring "the possibility of freedom and justice . . . ." Discussing diverse experiences and motivations at a variety of levels, she concludes, "the preservation of memory is common to all liberation theologies. . . . Such memories are an affirmation of human dignity." The Afrocentric reading of Psalm 68 carries such a dangerous memory and serves as an alternative, insurrectionary, and subversive knowledge that confronts the moral failure of racial oppression.

Peter Paris has examined the translation of this claim to be children of God into a normative tradition within black churches. He found that, "[What] . . . has always been normative for the black churches and the black community . . . is that tradition governed by the principle of nonracism . . . . The fundamental principle . . . is depicted most adequately in the *biblical* doctrine of the parenthood of God and the kinship of all peoples--which is a version of the traditional sexist expression 'the Fatherhood of God and the brotherhood of men.' " In order to affirm the integrity of their communities and to counter the disruption of their families, black people corrected this exclusion by extending the role of God the Father to that of "Mother to the Motherless." All peoples are then included as male and female *experiences of suffering*. Paris concludes, "The principle of freedom and equality of all persons under God is not an abstract idea but a normative condition of the black churches, wherein all who participate can experience its reality." While it is tempting to attribute the welcome white people receive to white-skin privilege, this ignores the active defiance of racial segregation that is part of black churches' history. The utilization of Psalm 68, then, represents an important strategy in the construction of this nonracist appropriation of Christianity. It provides authority for the "Ethiopians" to "sing the Lord's song in a strange land" and to create a "House of Prayer for All People," the name of one twentieth century black religious movement that preached racial equality. Acknowledging God as a "mother to the motherless" plants an incipient although unelaborated anti-sexist Christianity as well.

Along with its anti-racism, the reference to Ethiopia has laid the foundation for varieties of black Christian nationalism. Churches named themselves "Ethiopian," "African," or "Abyssinian." Some have used "Ethiopia" to argue for the economic, political, and social self-interest and solidarity in the context of the Christian ethic of love. C.L. Franklin used the text to criticize the militant masculinism of the rhetoric of black power ("I'm a man!"). Franklin admonished his listeners to be "children"--children of God.

In a racist society that is specifically anti-black and anti-African, Psalm 68 enables black people to claim their African identity. Furthermore, it asserts humanity and community where oppressors try to strip away ethnic identity and assault community in order to extract the greatest possible wealth. Psalm 68:31 authorizes universal siblinghood in relation to an all-powerful and decidedly partial God. God's partiality for the poor, the oppressed, and the captive carries a call to privileged elder siblings to be responsible members of the human family. The prophetic apocalyptic connection of this psalm sees redemption or salvation as social liberation.

Brueggemann (1984) argues that the hermeneutics of experience govern the way in which psalms should be classified. Since Longman finds Psalm 68 comparable to Psalms 29, 47, 96, 98, 114, and 124, Psalm 68 can be classified as a "community thanksgiving" or a "victory-enthronement song." Brueggemann (1984:134-52) calls these "psalms of new orientation." Such songs, "are . . . about the decisive *transformation* made possible by this God who causes new life where none seems possible." These psalms of new orientation "offer a variety of solutions in a continuum of continuity and discontinuity." They "regularly bear witness to the surprising gift of new life just when none had been expected. . . . Since Israel cannot explain and refuses to speculate, it can do what it does best. It can tell, narrate, recite, testify, in amazement and gratitude, 'lost in wonder, love, and praise.' " The reference to "Ethiopia" provides the special permission black Christians need to place themselves in what Brueggemann calls "Jewish territory" and to be included not only at the end of the story in the final victory of God, but also at the beginning of the story--*before* their oppressors preached "slaves obey your masters." Black Christians' song of new orientation becomes, "How I got over!/How I got over!/You know my soul looks back and wonders;/How I got over!" (Ward). The daily prayer of new orientation can be, "I thank God for waking me up this morning, clothed in my right mind, and with the blood running warm in my body."

In a context of powerlessness and oppression, there is a substantial theological point that is " . . . also a sociopolitical one; it is the triumph of the *power of liberation* over the *power of control* (Brueggemann, 1984:137)." These songs state "which god is the real God," and they provide a powerful alternative to the oppressive anglocentric reading that justified slavery. For the Afro-Christian tradition, the psalm was a simple statement, later echoed in the hymn of C.A. Tindley, "There is a God who rules above/With hand of power and heart of love;/If I am right, He'll fight my battle;/I shall be free some day." This Afrocentric reading lays the foundation for affirming the person/peoplehood of Africans and their descendents. It is also a profound statement of hope. Such a reading includes black people as an oppressed people in the primary liberating acts of God and recognizes clearly the problem of a people who are poor, in chains, and solitary.

It is important, then, to speculate on the cultural imagination that enabled the agents of the Afro-Christian tradition to expand upon the image of God as "A father of the fatherless." As a locus of meaning and as a fertile space for religious imagination and synthesis, Psalm 68 points in a subtle way to issues central in the reconstruction of a world view in a context of oppression and resistance. In speaking to the issue of gender, this Afrocentric reading, by expanding upon the text, anticipates a central problem of the contemporary church. It identified the role of women as important religious substance in a context of racial oppression. In grappling with images of power it spoke to the importance of a powerful God while at the same time placing the "motherly" alongside of the "fatherly." The importance of the Psalm in legitimizing black people's appropriation of the Bible for their religious life, in the face of their owners' corrupt readings, also drew connections with the problem of community integrity, family disruption, and ethnic (i.e., African) identity. Finally, its reading of the once and future place of Ethiopia in the sanctuary of God underscored the tension between the here and now and the "after while, bye and bye"; the traditional utilization of the psalm represents an important example of the way in which an activist hope is nurtured within black religion.

Gender, Imagery, and the Black Experience

The use of any traditional image of God carries with it a reflection of the people who utilize that image in worship and in everyday social life. Feminist critiques of God-talk have pointed to the use of the Bible and its masculine language as a reflection and reinforcement of the male-over-female character of contemporary society. Black people learned of God as "a father of the fatherless" through patriarchal imagery in an androcentric text. Furthermore, the social category or term "motherless" is nowhere to be found in the King James Version. However, black people were not without biblical authority in viewing God as female, particularly mother.

Biblical feminists, particularly Mollenkott, point to the abundance of female imagery in the Bible and the failure of Christian tradition to draw upon that imagery when representing God in the preaching and other symbolic constructions. In the prophetic texts, God repeatedly reveals God's self in a variety of maternal activities: "as the one who carries, feeds, protects, heals, guides, disciplines, comforts, washes, and clothes her human children" (Mollenkott:27). In addition to these maternal activities, there are five explicit biblical revelations of God as mother. First there is the mother giving birth.

> Not only is the Creator depicted as carrying in the womb or birthing creation, but also Christ and the Holy Spirit are depicted in similar roles. . . . God's anguish at the human failure

to embody justice is captured in the image of a woman writhing, unable to catch her breath in the pain of her travail. This image makes God seem very much present alongside all those who are oppressed by the turmoil and suffering of our world (Mollenkott:15).

Additionally, Mollenkott demonstrates that there is God as nursing mother in Isaiah 49:15, Psalm 34:9, and Hosea 11:4 (20-25); we find God as a mother bear in Hosea 13:8 (47-53); God is revealed as mother eagle in Deuteronomy 32:11-12 and Exodus 19:4 (83-91); and God is found as mother hen in Matthew 23:27 and Luke 13:34 (92-96).

The mother images of God have found their way into the traditions of Africans and Afro-Americans. One finds creation as an act of giving birth in some African cosmologies. God as mother eagle, ironically enough, is found in the most masculine and androcentric dimensions of Afro-Christian worship--its preaching (Gilkes:82-87). There is a large tradition of sermons all titled, "The Eagle Stirreth Her Nest." The image of God as mother is an important component of what "everybody knows" and takes for granted in the language of prayer, sermon, song, and testimony. During a nationally televised debate over the *Inclusive Language Lectionary*, a black woman member of the audience stated that for black people, God had always been "a mother to the motherless, and a father to the fatherless." She implied that this was a taken-for-granted, more or less common sense aspect of Afro-Christian religious knowledge. This motherly omnipotence attributed to God within the black tradition has been used as a corrective and reminder to those who would restrict the imagery of God to the realm of the male and who would forget the larger formulation, of paramount importance to the tradition, that "God is spirit." This perspective is part of the core of Afro-American religious knowledge.

The theological concerns of contemporary feminism have created a crisis surrounding traditional images of God in church and society. While creating a crisis in language, contemporary religious feminism sought to engage women in interracial and cross-cultural dialogues. In the development of those dialogues, it became apparent that black and white women in the United States view their respective religious traditions somewhat differently. White women pointed to the correspondence between biblical imagery and the position of all women in church and society. Furthermore, explicit justifications for patriarchal church structures which demanded that women be silent and invisible were important sources of anger and discontent for white women. The feminist critique that addressed this source of anger mobilized women to break silence and to attain visibility within their churches. As a result inclusive language is a prominent practical issue in today's church. The introduction to the first *Inclusive Language Lectionary* details the importance of this issue while the introduction to year C adds commentary on the severe difference of opinion that exists between black and white traditions concerning the use of the term "the Lord."

Black women argue that they face a different set of problems. While recognizing the patriarchal character of their churches, black women struggle primarily around their access to the pulpits of their largest denominations. Jacquelyn Grant provides a forceful discussion of this problem in her article "Black Women and the Church." In it she details the way in which both historical and contemporary black women preachers were barred from pulpits simply because they were women. She also notes her observations that women are kept from power in the larger more often than the smaller churches.

In spite of the conflict over preaching, black women were part of the language of their worship traditions from the beginning of their sojourn in the United States. Thomas Webber describes the "remarkable lack of sexism" that existed in the slave quarters community and the manner in which women leaders shaped the basic foundation of religious practice. Deborah Gray White (119-41) describes the female slave network as an important institution for the survival and resistance of slaves that stood alongside the family and religion in its importance for the survival of the slave community. This network provided the opportunity for black women to maintain autonomous religious rituals in the form of prayer meetings and for women to be influential leaders for the entire community. The integral role of women in the construction of a biblically grounded Afro-Christian tradition precluded the problem of silence and visibility.

Later black Christian women faced a progressive disempowerment. They were heard and seen but they were not proportionally represented in the pastoral offices that symbolized authority and power. Because of their historical importance to the symbolization process within black churches, black women did not identify biblical language as a principle source of their discontent. Prior to the emergence of contemporary feminism, black women's discontent took the form of conflicts over leadership within local churches and denominations that occasionally led to the formation of new congregations or denominations. To some extent, the familiar epithet, "If it wasn't for the women you wouldn't have a church," represented the endemic conflict over the role of women that has characterized black church politics from the late nineteenth century to the present. Black men and women agreed about the *importance* of women but not the *position* of women. Thus women and men shared the languages of worship in the Afro-Christian tradition in spite of their conflicts over structure and authority.

For Africans, reading the Bible as a text for liberation and hope presented some peculiar problems. A principle category of helplessness in the Bible is represented by the "fatherless." For people from West African cultures, the ultimate social tragedy was not fatherlessness but *motherlessness*. The importance of the social role of mother came through clearly in the religious representations that surrounded fertility and the offices reserved for women that extended the role of mother to the larger politics of gender and economic relations. Although patriarchal, the matrilineality and bilineality of African societies did not limit social identity and place to one portion of family relations. Marriage was important, fathers had great power and authority, but mothers represented the essential relationship for children and the mother-child relationship enjoyed a high degree of autonomy in the context of polygynous societies. To be a motherless child was the ultimate social tragedy. In contemporary times, unmarried women have been known to give up their children and some West African peoples refer to their orphanages as "motherless camps."

Matrilineal societies, as the literature on West Africa demonstrates, are more inclusive in their view of social roles although not necessarily less oppressive. Although we may argue about the degree of oppression experienced by women in such societies, the literature is clear in stating that the precolonial societies of West Africa accorded women relatively more power and authority than did western patriarchies (Clarke). The economic role of African women augmented their family roles and afforded them an avenue for exercising power within and beyond the family. As mothers, then, they were powerful figures whose power, if they were successful in the marketplace and were able to fit properly into the cooperative networks of other women, grew with age and experience. To be a child without such a mother and to be a society without such women, then, was a problem that surely required the attention of Heaven.

African women's roles as mother extended beyond household and clan. They were important mothers of civilization in their roles as political leaders. Some scholars argue that African women were the first women, historically, to emerge as queens of nations (Clarke:15). The oppression of the slave trade and colonialism included "a war on African customs, religion, and cultures. In most cases, the first custom they attacked was the matriarchy, attacks which increased after the Muslim invasion of Africa (Clarke:17)." Although direct memory of the militant role of African women in opposing the slave trade is difficult to argue, it is important to note that African traditions not only accorded women great visibility and autonomy but also contained strong models of female leadership. The tradition of prominent warrior queens, identified by various historians seems to have extended from

1500 B.C. until "the last of the major wars in Africa led by a woman" around 1900 A.D. Apparently, evidence for this tradition is found all over the continent.

The experience of Africans in America was to observe the destruction of systems of motherly honor and female power. The drama of this devastation can be found in the sorrow song's lament: "Sometimes I feel like a *motherless* child; . . . / A long way from home." In spite of the biblical emphasis on the tragedy of fatherlessness, the slaves sang about motherlessness. The religious tradition became a vehicle through which the dangerous memories of motherlessness were ritually remembered. Not only did people sing about being "a motherless child," but they described the depression related to their suffering: "I've been 'buked and I've been scorned;/ . . . I've been talked about sure as you're born" or "Sometimes I'm up, sometimes I'm down;/Oh yes, Lord./Sometimes I'm almost to the ground;/Oh yes, Lord" or "Sometime I feel like I'm almost gone; a long way from home." In such oppressed circumstances, one had to ask the prophet's chariot to "Swing low, sweet chariot."

Their Afrocentric reading of Psalm 68, then, understood that any restoration to power and personhood involved the restoration of the lost mothers of civilization. For Africans, a disinterested Father-God would represent the transcendent Creator whose African antecedents were somewhat deistic in their relationships with their children. An attraction of Christianity was the reconciling role of Jesus that replaced a complicated structure of ancestors and deities in linking the concerns of humankind with the Divine. Since Africans in Africa also prayerfully recognized the motherliness of God in Christ through Jesus's lament, "O Jerusalem, Jerusalem, thou that killest the prophets, and stonest them which are sent unto thee, how often would I have gathered thy children together, even as a hen gathereth her chickens under her wings, and ye would not!," it is not unreasonable to assume that the Africans in the New World grasped its importance also. It is quite possible that the spiritual "Rocking Jerusalem" reflects imaginatively on this text and indirectly links the discipleship of Mary and Martha to the role of God the Mother in Jesus, an interesting argument for the necessity of women's ordination to the priesthood. The fatherly image of God would represent a "hand of power" but would be incomplete without the "heart of love" that represented a more complete picture of African notions of power. Since motherliness was also equated with power, such imagery served a legitimizing function for an alternative, truly humane, view of power at the same time fatherly power was admonished to appropriate a model of intimate care and tenderness. A truly all-powerful God would incorporate both motherly and fatherly impotence.

Such an extension of the text to incorporate God's motherly omnipotence not only opposes the oppressive utilization of the Bible during and after slavery, but shapes the perceptions of gender within the community--perceptions in tension with the dominant culture. Afro-Christian culture remembered the heroism of its mothers along with that of its fathers and therefore constructed its myths, by extending the biblical materials provided, "in memory of her." These biblical theological images hold within them important memories of social roles and the honor accorded those social roles in the African and American experiences. It is important to uphold these inclusive images in order to prevent their destruction in reaction to their deviation from the larger society. This is an important voice in the cultural conflict between images of loving God (feminine) and images of a powerful warrior God (masculine) that is posed in the feminist revision of biblical language.

"Religious symbols formulate a basic congruence between a particular style of life and a specific (if, most often, implicit) metaphysic, and in so doing sustain each with the borrowed authority of the other (Geertz, 1973)." African Americans recognized almost intuitively the basic congruence between the religion of the "Blessed Book" and the lifestyle forced upon them as slaves. Taking seriously the liberation story basic to the book, they reverently manipulated the basic materials in order to fashion a faith that fit both their Sitz im Leben and the basic demands of biblical religion. Since their creative reverence involved fitting a patriarchal text to a world view full of bilineal descent and strong slave women, most of whom became mothers, there are important lessons to be found for the biblical feminist who seeks to remain faithful to the Bible as a foundation--an authoritative foundation--for faith, while rejecting a death dealing social order--the social order of contemporary patriarchy.

Dangerous Good News: Hope in an Afrocentric Biblical Tradition

The liberationist biblical voices within the contemporary Church represent significant subversive opposition to the powers, principalities, and rulers of the dark places of this world. Our fascination with the feminist and Third World voices sometimes overlooks the important contribution of the Afro-American biblical voice that stretches back over several centuries. The Afrocentric biblical tradition is an important witness to the persistence of dangerous memories and alternative knowledges in spite of the most formidable cultural pressures.

Every liberationist reading of the Bible is a response to oppression. These readings point to the intended news for the oppressed. The oppressions and victimizations of contemporary society are multiple and the victims are diverse. Victimization and oppression in this society are usually accompanied by corrupt and ideologized readings of the Bible. The symbolic importance of the Bible in the struggle for social justice cannot be ignored. Liberationist hermeneutics present formidable social challenges since they emerge at the cutting edges of human suffering.

As a liberationist reading, the Afrocentric biblical tradition apprehends the suffering experienced because of racial oppression. Black people managed to extend their theologizing to include the suffering of the majority of the community, *women*. Contrary to conventional sociohistorical wisdom, this reading reached back into African cultural memory to affirm the importance of the feminine as part of African cosmology (Gleason), the history of the roles of African women as leaders and agents of communal integrity, and the continuities of these women's roles within the slave community. What has been done in the past, using Psalm 68 as only one example, represents a strategy for the cultural production of hope in oppressive and *depressing* circumstances.

Apprehending gender as an important category of experience in which God reveals God's self is dangerous good news. This Afrocentric tradition with its affirmations of God as "mother to the motherless," "sister to the sisterless," "Solomon's Rose of Sharon" and its vividly sung memories of "Mary and Martha" provides an opportunity to reclaim the Bible as a foundation for women's spirituality. Not only does it affirm black experience in a context that is anti-black, anti-African, and anti-female, but this view of God maintains the connection with the divine feminine in a masculinized *Protestant* context. In a society that is also anti-Catholic, the connections with female saints and with Mary, the mother of Jesus, have been lost as authoritative expressions of women's experience as a gift to the Church. Boff's (2) recent work argues that "the question of the feminine has acquired great importance in our time." He states, "Our culture is engaged in a tremendous reappraisal of the intuitive, of the feminine, of everything affecting or concerning subjectivity. . . . . Within the institutional framework of the powers that be, the image of God flashes forth with a new face." He then goes on to ask, "Can we regard God as our Mother as well as our Father?"

The Afrocentric biblical tradition responds affirmatively and sees this "new face" as an "old face" in African cosmology and in Afro-Christian tradition. Not only can we regard God as our Mother as well as our Father, we can redefine the boundaries of motherhood and fatherhood, demanding that men emulate the tenderness of God as nursing mother and affirming the right of women to an assertiveness that defends, protects, changes, brings justice, and gives birth to a better world.

The Afrocentric biblical tradition *heritagizes* the black experience for other suffering communities of believers while maintaining its particularities as a gift to the Church; it transforms its experiences into a sacred story from which *religion* can be constructed and passed on. In one sense, this Afrocentric tradition is a canonical-critical perspective that has grown up in the heart of American racial oppression. This tradition tries to extract from ". . . the Bible the unrecorded hermeneutics that lie between so many lines of it (Sanders, 1987:186)." As an extension of the "theocentric monotheizing hermeneutic" that Sanders identifies as the prevalent and "consistent" motive force in the construction of biblical canon, the Afrocentric approach furnishes a prophetic-apocalyptic extension that re-visions that canon from a christocentric and anthropocentric point of view. It is a hermeneutical matrix for the liberationist redevelopment of biblical religion in an oppressive society.

In closing, Houston Baker reminds us that our central task as students of the Afro-American experience is one of reconstruction. Using the metaphor of the railroad track, he argues "It is essential . . . when talking of 'reconstruction' to decide first whether any . . . used crossties are worth salvaging in attempts to create a new perspective." The Afro-Christian reading of the King James Bible is a complex phenomenon. The fragments or "crossties" of this special cultural imagination are in the songs, prayers, testimonies, and sermons. These special crossties, commended fragments of the King James Bible, direct us to a significant hermeneutical gift for the historical project of human liberation.

---

*An earlier version was presented to the American Academy of Religion and Society of Biblical Literature Annual Meeting; December 7, 1987; Boston, Massachusetts; Women in the Biblical World Section. I wish to acknowledge Rev. Gardner C. Taylor's descriptions of the importance of Psalm 68 in the communities of his youth and Professor George MacRae's encouragement to explore the Afro-American tradition of Bible reading. My colleague, Thomas Longstaff, made a number of helpful comments and provided insights into the Anglican prayer tradition. I am very grateful to those members of the Boxford, Massachusetts Volunteer Fire Department who rescued an early and only draft of this paper along with the research notes from my burning car.

WORKS CONSULTED

Anderson, Bernhard
    1983   *Out of the Depths: The Psalms Speak for Us Today*. Philadelphia: Westminster.

Asante, Molefi Kete
    1987   *The Afrocentric Idea*. Philadelphia: Temple University Press.

Baker, Houston A., Jr.
    1984   *Blues, Ideology, and Afro-American Literature: A Vernacular Theory*. Chicago: University of Chicago Press.

Bartel, Rolad, with James Ackerman and Thayer S. Warshaw, eds.
    1975   *Biblical Images in Literature*. Nashville: Abingdon.

Blassingame, John W.
    1979   *The Slave Community: Plantation Slavery in the Antebellum South*, 2nd ed. New York: Oxford University Press.

Boff, Leonardo, O.F.M.
    1987   *The Maternal Face of God: The Feminine and Its Religious Expressions*. San Francisco: Harper and Row.

Brewster, Herbert
    1949   "Our God Is Able." P. 1 in *Golden Gospel Songs: Volume 1*. Chicago: Martin Morris Music, Inc.

Briggs, Charles Augustus and Emilie Grace Briggs
    1907   *A Critical and Exegetical Commentary on the Books of Psalms*, ICC 2. New York: Scribner's.

Brueggemann, Walter
    1982   *Praying the Psalms*. Winona, Minnesota: Saint Mary's Press.
    1984   *The Message of the Psalms: A Theological Commentary*. Minneapolis: Augsburg.

Buttrick, David G.
    1987   *Homiletic: Moves and Structures*. Philadelphia: Fortress.

Carter, Harold
    1976   *The Prayer Tradition of Black People*. Valley Forge, Pennsylvania: Judson.

Clarke, John Henrik
    1975   "The Black Woman in History." *The Black World* Feb.:12-26.

Cone, James
    1972   *The Spirituals and the Blues: An Interpretation*. New York: Seabury.

Dahood, Mitchell
    1968   *Psalms II: 51-100*. The Anchor Bible, 17. Garden City, New York: Doubleday.

DuBois, W.E.B.
    1970   *The Gift of Black Folk: The Negroes in the Making of America*. New York: Simon and Schuster (original publication date, 1921).

Franklin, C.L.
    n.d.   "The Meaning of Black Power." New York: Chess/Janus Records.

Geertz, Clifford
    1973   "Religion as a Cultural System." Pp. 87-125 in *The Interpretation of Cultures: Selected Essays*. New York: Basic Books.

Gilkes, Cheryl Townsend
    1987   "'Some Mother's Son and Some Father's Daughter': Gender and Biblical Language in Afro-Christian Worship Tradition." Pp. 73-99 in *Shaping New Vision: Gender and Values in American Culture*. Ed. Clarissa W. Atkinson, Constance H. Buchanan, and Margaret R. Miles. Ann Arbor, Michigan: UMI Research Press.

Gleason, Judith
    1987   *Oya: In Praise of the Goddess*. Boston Shambhala Publications.

Grant, Jacquelyn
    1982   "Black Women and the Church." Pp. 141-152 in *But Some of Us Are Brave: Black Women's Studies*. Old Westbury, New York: The Feminist Press.

Gray, J.
    1977   "A Cantata of the Autumn Festival: Psalm lxviii." *JSS* 22:2-26.

Hanks, Thomas D.
    1983   *God So Loved the Third Word: The Bible, the Reformation, and Liberation Theologies*. Maryknoll, New York: Orbis.

Heilbut, Anthony
    1975   *The Gospel Sound: Good News and Bad Times.* New York: Simon and Schuster.

Hoppe, Leslie J.
    1984   Abstract of A. Tronina, "'Slady Tradycji Synajskie; w Ps. 68." *Old Testament Abstracts* 7:263.

Johnson, James Weldon
    1927   *God's Trombones: Seven Negro Sermons in Verse.* New York: Viking.

Lincoln, C. Eric
    1984   *Race, Religion, and the Continuing American Dilemma.* New York: Hill and Wang.

Litwack, Leon F.
    1979   *Been In the Storm So Long: The Aftermath of Slavery.* New York: Random House.

Long, Charles H.
    1986   *Significations: Signs, Symbols, and Images in the Interpretation of Religion.* Philadelphia: Fortress.

Longman, Tremper, III
    1984   "Psalm 98: A Divine Warrior Victory Song." *Journal of the Evangelical Theological Society* 27:267-74.

Mitchell, Henry
    1970   *Black Preaching.* New York: Harper and Row.
    1977   *The Recovery of Preaching.* New York: Harper and Row.

Mollenkott, Virginia Ramey
    1983   *The Divine Feminine: The Biblical Imagery of God as Female.* New York: Crossroad.

National Council of Churches
    1983   *Inclusive Language Lectionary: Year A.* Boston: Pilgrim.
    1984   *Inclusive Language Lectionary: Year B.* Boston: Pilgrim.
    1985   *Inclusive Language Lectionary: Year C.* Boston: Pilgrim.

Paris, Peter J.
    1985   *The Social Teaching of the Black Churches.* Philadelphia: Fortress.

Patterson, Orlando
1982   *Slavery and Social Death: A Comparative Study*. Cambridge, Massachusetts: Harvard University Press.

Raboteau, Albert
1978   *Slave Religion: The "Invisible Institution" in the Antebellum South*. New York: Oxford University Press.

Richardson, Marilyn, ed.
1987   *Maria W. Stewart, America's First Black Woman Political Writer: Essays and Speeches*. Bloomington: Indiana University Press.

Sanders, James A.
1984   *Canon and Community: A Guide to Canonical Criticism*. Philadelphia: Fortress.
1987   *From Sacred Story to Sacred Text: Canon as Paradigm*. Philadelphia: Fortress.

Schildenberger, Johannes
198   "Psalm 68. Gott inmitten seines Volkes," *Erbe and Auftrag*.

Schüssler Fiorenza, Elisabeth
1983   *In Memory of Her: A Feminist Theological Reconstruction of Christian Origins*. New York: Crossroad.
1984   *Bread not Stone: The Challenge of Feminist Biblical Interpretation*. Boston: Beacon.

Schüssler Fiorenza, Elisabeth and Mary Collins, eds.
1985   *Women--Invisible in Theology and Church*. Concilium 182(6). Edinburgh: T.T. Clark.

Shorter, Alyward
1975   *Prayer in the Religious Traditions of Africa*. New York: Oxford University Press.

Sobel, Mechal
1979   *Trabelin' On: The Slave Journey to an Afro-Baptist Faith*. Westport, Connecticut: Greenwood.

Sterling, Dorothy
1984   *We Are Your Sisters: Black Women in the Nineteenth Century*. New York: W.W. Norton.

Stuckey, Sterling
1987   *Slave Culture: Nationalist Theory and the Foundations of Black America*. New York: Oxford University Press.

Tamez, Elsa
1982   *Bible of the Oppressed.* Maryknoll, New York: Orbis.

Taylor, William R.
1955   "Exegesis Psalm 68," Pp. 353-61 in *The Interpreter's Bible.* Vol. 4. New York: Abingdon.

Thurman, Howard
1979   *With Head and Heart: The Autobiography of Howard Thurman.* New York: Harcourt Brace Jovanovich.

Tindley, C.A.
1905   "Someday," P. 27 in *Soul Echoes: A Collection of Songs for Religious Meetings.* Philadelphia: Union.

Tronina, A.
1982   " 'Slady Tradycji Synajskiej w Ps. 68." *Roczniki Teol.-Kanoniczne* 29:45-51.

Walker, Wyatt Tee
1979   *Somebody's Calling My Name: Black Sacred Music and Social Change.* Valley Forge, Pennsylvania: Judson.

Ward, Clara
1951   "How I Got Over." Philadelphia: Andrea Music Company. P. 188 in *Songs of Zion.* Nashville: Abingdon. 1981.

Ward Singers
1978   "The Best of the Ward Singers of Philadelphia, Pennsylvania." Elizabeth, New Jersey. Savoy Records.

Webber, Thomas
1976   *Deep Like the Rivers: Education in the Slave Quarter Community, 1831-1865.* New York: W.W. Norton.

Welch, Sharon D.
1985   *Communities of Resistance and Solidarity: A Feminist Theology of Liberation.* Maryknoll, New York: Orbis.

Westermann, Claus
1980   *The Psalms: Structure, Content, and Message.* Minneapolis: Augsburg.

White, Deborah Gray
1985   *Ar'n't I A Woman? Female Slaves in the Plantation South.* New York: W.W. Norton.

Williams, Chancellor
    1974   *The Destruction of Black Civilization.* Chicago: Third World Press.

Wilmore, Gayraud
    1983   *Black Religion and Black Radicalism: An Interpretation of the Religious History of Afro-American People.* Maryknoll, New York: Orbis.

Yoffre, Horatio Simian
    1981   "La teodicea del Deuteroisaias." *Biblica* 62:55-72.

GOMER: VICTIM OF VIOLENCE OR VICTIM OF METAPHOR?*

Renita J. Weems
Vanderbilt Divinity School

ABSTRACT

Hosea's ingenious use of the marriage metaphor to describe the nature of YHWH and Israel's relationship provides special insight into divine-human relations. While it functions as a very effective literary device, it raises serious hermeneutical problems for those who are concerned about biblical texts that may be interpreted as excusing violence against women. In the case of the Hebrew Scriptures, to the extent that divine retribution is based on the presumably sound theological notion that the deity has the right to punish the people, the image of a husband physically retaliating against his wife becomes almost unavoidable, and his right to do so unquestionable. Following an introduction in which some hermeneutical issues are raised, there is a detailed exegesis of Hosea 2:4-25, with special attention to the image of sexual violence in the judgment speeches. Finally, after a discussion of the insights and limitations of the marriage metaphor, this study will conclude with remarks on the importance of and the hermeneutical issues at stake in having a diversity of metaphors to talk about the human-divine relationship.

In order to persuade listeners of the gravity of one's message, the first task of a prophet is to arrest the imagination of one's audience. To convince Israel of her urgent need to repent of her covenant unfaithfulness, the eighth century prophet Hosea made use of a myriad of poetic images to capture in various ways the nature of YHWH's affection for and claims upon Israel and to portray the depth of Israel's estrangement from YHWH.[1] Of the fourteen or more images that he used to

---

[1] (1) marriage and harlotry (chaps. 1-3; *passim*); (2) Israel like a stubborn heifer/trained heifer (4:16 and 10:11); (3) YHWH like a moth and dry rot (5:12); (4) YHWH as lion (5:14); (5) Israel's love like morning dew (6:4) and the reversal where YHWH becomes dew to Israel (14:5); (6) Israel like a silly dove and YHWH a waiting net (7:11-12); (7) YHWH as a vulture (8:1); (8) Israel like sin-filled altars (8:11); (9) Israel like grapes in the wilderness (9:10); (10) Israel like a flourishing vine (10:1; 14:7);

characterize Israel and YHWH's relationship, however, no other one in the Hoseanic corpus has attracted a greater amount of attention from scholars than Hosea's comparison of the covenantal bond between YHWH and faithless Israel to that of his marital relation with the ʾēšet zĕnûnîm Gomer. Given the fact that the marital-harlotry motif dominates the prologue to the book (chaps. 1-3) and its theme is alluded to throughout the remaining eleven chapters of the book, it is probably safe to say that the image loomed large as well in the mind of the prophet (or that of his editors).

In the past, scholars have been preoccupied with the historical questions that such an alleged marriage proposes (e.g. the laws regarding Hebrew marriage and divorce,[2] the nature of Canaanite fertility cults and their penetration into Hebrew religious practices,[3] the fascinating account of Hosea and Gomer's alleged stormy marriage[4]). Only recently have scholars begun to take note of the peculiarly literary nature and function of the first three chapters of Hosea.[5] Thanks to the pioneering efforts of critics like L. Alonso-Schokel (1960, 1975, 1983), James Muilenburg (1969) and others, in recent years more and more scholars are beginning to acknowledge that (1) meaning cannot be abstracted from form, (2) the meaning of a text is as much, if not more so, a function of its form and structure as it is its content, and (3) in fact, one must be careful about the kinds of historical questions one poses to the texts (and especially the historical conclusions that are drawn as a result) given the chiefly literary makeup of the texts. These maxims apply particularly to poetry, which characterizes the bulk of prophetic material. A fundamental feature of poetry is its metaphorical nature; and the fact that it is metaphorical, in many instances, mitigates against one's ability to adduce precise historical data. This is certainly true of Hosea where, given the highly emotional level of the speeches, the language tends not to be always coherent and logical, but more often evocative and ambiguous. As J. Cheryl Exum (333) has pointed out, poetry is by its nature ambiguous or "plurisignificant," meaning that "its power derives from its ability to

---

(11) Israel as YHWH's son (11:1-12); (12) YHWH like a tearing lion (13:7); (13) Israel like a reed in the face of the wind (13:15); (14) YHWH like an evergreen cypress (14:8).

[2]See, e.g., L.M. Muntingh.

[3]Herbert G. May's article is the most classic example of this line of inquiry.

[4]For a fine summary of the various, and in some instances eccentric, reconstructions of the prophet's marriage that have been adduced from chaps. 1-3, see H.H. Rowley.

[5]In addition to being a much needed improvement over the predominantly diachronic interests of older commentaries by Wolff, J. Mays, and Rudolph, the Anchor Bible commentary on Hosea by Francis Andersen and David N. Freedman provides a fine example of scholarship that exhibits unusual sensitivity to the overall literary integrity of the book while holding in tandem the historical issues that form its background. For examples of studies which are decidedly synchronic in approach, see W. Vogels and Henry Krszyna.

be suggestive of multiple meanings." This is not to argue that poetry has no basis in reality. For as difficult as it may be for the modern reader to imagine YHWH commanding someone to do so, there is no reason to doubt that a marriage took place between the prophet Hosea and the zônâ Gomer. Further, assuming there ever was such a marriage, neither do we have reason to doubt that the details of Hosea's marriage to Gomer conformed to the laws governing and the reality of eighth century Hebrew marriages. In other words (and this is important to stress), attention to form and structure is not to discount or ignore *a priori* diachronic interests in the text, where questions about the history that the text attests to predominate. Instead, the premise of this study is, laying aside questions as to whether or not a marriage even took place and the details of Hebrew marriage customs or foreign fertility rites, there are important insights to be gained by respecting first the prophet's message as it has been transmitted to us as a literary work.[6]

Moreover, not only have scholars neglected the peculiarly literary character of the material in Hosea, they have also failed to consider in any substantial way the significance of Hosea's[7] use of sexual imagery and gynomorphic language to describe the volatile character of the divine-human relationship.[8] To be sure, the most useful function of this kind of language is its highly emotive impact. For what was the case in ancient Israel remains the case in modern times: talk about sex and sexuality tends to provoke, rouse, humiliate, and captivate people. Such language certainly arrests the imagination.[9]

Nonetheless, having concluded that the strength of this kind of imagery is its emotive effects and that at the center of the motif is the effort to convey the notion that YHWH and Israel's relationship is like that of a marital union between a man and woman, the contention here is that biblical theologians must go a step further and consider the

---

[6] Literary analysis and historical analysis as discrete methodological categories are not as mutually exclusive as some scholarly quarters seem to imply. In the best studies, like that of Andersen/Freedman, they mutually inform each other. For there are many instances, even in Hosea, in which historical findings can help to adjudicate literary issues and conversely a sensitivity to a text's literary persona can help shed light on historical questions.

[7] Although the marital-harlotry motif appears elsewhere in the Old Testament, most notably Jeremiah and Ezekiel, Hosea appears to be the first of the canonical prophets to employ such an image. Of course, as Moshe Weinfeld has pointed out, such a concept was probably already latent, though not explicit, in the ancient Pentateuchal concept of covenant (81, 6).

[8] As a notable exception to this, Robert Carroll deserves to be highly commended for, among other things, what certainly has to be one of the most forthright and sensitive examinations of the ribald sexual language and imagery of the prophet Jeremiah, the latter who was in many ways influenced by Hosea's language and theology.

[9] For a helpful discussion of those places throughout the Hebrew Bible where such imagery occurs and the emotive impact of such imagery, see David J. Clark.

consequences of such biblical imagery.[10] The present study, therefore, which concerns itself with Hosea's use of the marriage metaphor to describe Israel's relationship to YHWH, argues two things. First, as a literary device the metaphor provides *particular* insight into the nature of YHWH and Israel's relationship in ways that other Hoseanic metaphors cannot. Second, even though the marriage metaphor serves as an effective literary device, to the extent that it depends on the image of the sexual abuse of a woman to develop and defend its point, as a dominant theological model the marriage metaphor is limited, if not risky.

In the first chapter of Hosea we find YHWH's command to the prophet Hosea to marry the "unfaithful woman"[11] Gomer. Oddly, the prophet obeys this unparalleled command without question. We learn also in chap. 1 of the children born from that union, Jezreel, Not-Pitied, and Not-My-People, whose names are symbolic of Israel's estrangement from YHWH. In chap. 3, having forgiven his wife her indiscretions and unfaithfulness, Hosea now takes the necessary measures to restore his marriage, his actions signifying YHWH's own amazing pardoning love toward a recalcitrant people *lēk ʾĕhab ʾiššā(h) ʾăhūbt rēaʿ ūmĕnāʾāpet kĕʾahăbat yĕhwāh ʾet bĕnê yiśrāʾēl* (v. 1). Here again we observe the obedient prophet acting without protest on behalf of the deity. These two chapters, however, fail to provide the reader with any clue as to what the prophet felt about what he was commanded to do, or how he felt about the woman Gomer. Moreover, one gets the impression that the woman Gomer quietly acquiesced to Hosea's overtures. Whereas the first and third chapters open and close with the image of Hosea's faithful obedience (YHWH's steadfast love, by analogy), in chap. 2, fortunately, the reader gets a glance into what was in fact the stormy nature of the prophet and his wife's relationship. Chap. 2, therefore, serves as a dramatic poetic centerpiece in the prologue of chaps. 1-3. Here the poetry moves with varying intensity back and forth

---

[10]In short, as a feminist biblical scholar, this writer is concerned about motifs and texts which rely upon the physical and sexual abuse of a *woman* to develop its larger, presumably congenial, theological point about divine love and retribution. As a black and womanist biblical scholar the writer is concerned about motifs and texts which rely upon the physical and sexual exploitation of *anyone* to develop its larger, presumably congenial theological point.

[11]There has been a considerable amount of debate around the correct translation of *ʾšt znwnym* in Hosea 1:2. Translators who are concerned, and rightly so, to capture the historical ramifications behind the word have translated the word "cult prostitute wife of harlotry" (Fensham), "wife of whoredom" (Wolff), "wife of promiscuity" (Andersen/Freedman) and the like. Clearly as one commentator has pointed out, this is a case where the practice and the metaphor overlap. Although the expression *ēšet zĕnūnîm* certainly carries strong sexual connotations, the intentionally neutral translation "unfaithful woman" is preferred here and is consistent, this writer believes, with the overall interest of the text. For a helpful discussion of the issues involved, see Andersen/Freedman (157-167).

throughout, bouncing back and forth between husband, wife and YHWH, dramatizing the bitter exchange between a husband and wife, and by analogy, YHWH and Israel. Here the details of the metaphor unfold. Here, also, one discovers the metaphor's versatility.

STROPHE I
2:4 "Reason with your mother, Reason [with her]—
    for is she not my wife
    and am I not her husband?
Let her remove her signs of unfaithfulness
    from her face
    and her evidence of adultery
    from between her breasts.
2:5 Lest I strip her naked,
    and make her as the day she was born,
    and make her like the wilderness,
    and change her into an arid land,
    and kill her with thirst.
2:6 Her children, I will not pity—
    because children born out of her
    unfaithfulness are they.
2:7 For their mother was (sexually) unfaithful,
    and gave birth in shame,
When she said, 'Let me go after my lovers,
    those who provide me my bread, my water,
    my wool, my flax, my oil and my liquor.'

STROPHE II
2:8 Therefore I will block her way with thorns;
    and hem her in with a wall,
    such that she will not be able to find
    her way.
2:9 If she pursues after her lovers,
    she will not overtake them.
    If she seeks them out, she will not find [them].
[Then] will she say,
    'Let me return to my first husband,
    for it was better for me then than now.

STROPHE III
2:10 She herself did not know that it was I who gave her the
    grain, the wine, and the oil,
and lavished upon her silver and gold which they

used for Baal.
2:11 Therefore, I will take back my grain in due time,
and my wine at the appointed time,
and will remove my wool and flax
which covers her nakedness.
2:12 Now I will expose her private parts
before her lovers' eyes.
And no one will be able to rescue her from my hands.
2:13 And I will put an end to all her festivities, her feasts,
her celebrations of the new moon,
and all her appointed celebrations.
2:14 And I will lay waste her vines and her fig trees
which she said,
'These are the gifts
my lovers gave to me.'

2:15 And I will punish her for the feast days of the Baals
wherein she burned incense to them
and adorned herself with her ring and her
her jewelry
and went after her lovers
but me she forgot,"
says the Lord.

STROPHE IV
2:16 "Then, behold, I will seduce her
and bring her into the wilderness
and speak romantically to her heart.
2:17 And there I will give to her her vineyards;
and the Valley of Achor will become
a door of hope.
And there she will answer as in the days of her youth,
as in the days when she came up
from the land of Egypt.
2:18 So will it be on that day,"
says the Lord.
"You will call me, 'My Husband'
and no longer will you call me,
'My Baal.'
2:19 I will remove the names of the Baals
from her mouth,
and they will no longer be mentioned by name.

STROPHE V

2:20 And I will make a covenant with them on that day,
    with the living things of the fields,
    with the fish of the sea,
    and the crawling things of the earth.
Bow, sword, and weapons of war,
    I will wipe out of the land.
And I will make them lie down in confidence.

2:21 And I will betroth you to me eternally.
I will betroth you to me in righteousness,
    justice, faithfulness,
    and in compassion.

2:22 I will betroth you to me in truth,
    and you will know YHWH.

2:23 And on that day,
    I will respond,"
    says YWHW.
"I will respond to the heavens,
    and they will respond to the earth.

2:24 And the land will respond to the grain and must and oil;
And they will answer Jezreel.

2:25 And I will sow it for myself in the land,
    and will show compassion
        upon the one who is not pitied.
And I will say to 'Not-My-People',
    'My People, you are'.
And he will say, 'My God.'"[12]

No other book in the Old Testament, except perhaps Jeremiah with whom Hosea curiously shares many features, resists easy literary analysis (i.e. isolating discrete units, perceiving principles of organization, identifying speakers) as does the book of Hosea. The common scholarly criteria for marking the beginning and end of a poem is, among other things, the presence of an imperative, the change of address or theme, the introduction of the oracular formula ("Thus says YHWH . . .") or a shift from poetry to prose. In a book such as Hosea where pronouns can change from one verse to another, themes are erratic, and, compared to other prophetic books, the oracular formula is rarely found, there is considerable diversity among scholars about how to divide up the poems.[13] This study concurs with those who isolate 2:4-

---

[12]This is the writer's own translation.

[13]For example, on the grounds that it is consistently a first person address with overall thematic consistency Anderson/Freedman (116-131) and Martin Buss (34) speak of 2:4-25 as a discrete poem. This is the case even though a thematic shift takes place in 2:20

25 as a discrete poem. The contention is that the imperative in 2:4 marks an important shift in both tone and address from the preceding verses, a shift from a third person narrative to a first person speech. The speech opens with the husband's appeal to his children, presumably Jezreel, Not-Pitied, and Not-My-People (1:3-8), to join him in his efforts to "reason" with their mother. This first person address concludes with v. 25 where the envisioned reconciliation between husband and wife brings with it harmony within the broader (ecological) family as denoted and echoed in the wordplay on the children's names, v. 24 *yizrěʿel*, v. 25 *lōʾ rūḥāmā(h) lōʾ ʿammî*.

Regarding the poem's organization, one clue is the use of quotations.[14] In chaps. 1 and 3, the prophet takes great pain to quote YHWH (1:1,2,4,6,8; 3:1). In 2:4-25 the prophet takes great pain to quote his wife: 2:7 *kî ʾomrā(h)*, 2:9 *wěʾomrā(h)*, and 2:14 *ʾăšher ʾomrā(h)*. The wife/Israel's claims (2:7,9,14) are summarized within the husband/YHWH's counterclaims and threats (2:8,10,15). In particular, at the center of their envisioned reconciliation is what the wife will correctly declare, "you will call me 'my husband,' " (2:18).[15] No longer will she incorrectly refer to him as 'my Baal.' In fact, all of the cosmos will join with the husband and wife in an exchange of vows where each will respond (*ʿānah*) to the other in a litany of love (2:20-25). This use of quotations for both human (2:7,9,14) and divine speech (2:15,18)[16] and the emphasis upon correct responses and declarations give strophic structure and unity to 2:4-25. The emphasis upon what has been said and what will be said gives the reader the impression that she or he is listening in on 1) a dialogue that is taking place between an irate husband and his stubborn wife 2:4-15, where the wife's erroneous claims (signifying Israel) are summarized in the husband's threatening counterclaims (signifying YHWH); and 2) a courtship scene between a man and a woman (2:16-25) where the former heaps lavish cosmic promises upon the latter in an effort to win her love and devotion.

This otherwise sentimental love drama would be touching were it not laced with threats of violence. The role that sexual violence plays in 2:4-25 and other biblical passages deserves far more attention than it

---

where particular allusions to the marriage, strife, and romance between husband and wife are abandoned and are replaced with language envisioning a broader eschatology. Such a vision of universal peace is reminiscent of 2:1-3. For this reason others like Hans Wolff (31-33) and Edwin Good (27-30), therefore, separate 2:4-17 from 2:18-25.

[14] For the use of quotations as a clue to perceiving the integrity of prophetic material, see John T. Willis.

[15] See Mordechai Friedman and A. Guillame.

[16] A further support to the suggestion that quotations serve as a key to understanding the structure of this poem is the fact that of the comparatively few instances in this book where the oracular formula nʾm yhwh occurs (2:15,18,23; 11:11), three of those four occurrences are within this poem.

is possible to give it here.[17] It is interesting to note that threats of violence also function to structure and shape this poem.

The poem opens in 2:4 with Hosea demanding (*rîbû*, the imperative) that the children intervene and reason with their mother. His tone is as much a plea as it is a command. After demanding that their children take up his case against his wife, the husband then lays out his formal complaint (vv. 4-7), laced throughout with his first set of threats (vv. 5-7). He charges that their marriage vows have been broken not only because of his wife's illicit sexual behavior, but also because she has wrongly and ignorantly ascribed to her lovers (*mᵉʾhby*) what rightfully belonged to her husband: the distinction of being the one to provide and care for her needs (vv. 7,10). In so doing, Gomer has made her lovers out to be her husband (*baʿĕlyî*) and gives to them what should have been her husband's alone, her loyalty and sexual intimacy. As a result, Hosea is very explicit about the punitive measures he is going to take. He threatens to strip her naked and kill her with thirst (v. 5). His second set of threats open with v. 8 where he threatens to barricade her with thorns and a wall, presumably, in her own home. And although she may submit for a while (v. 9), he tells himself, he knows that it will not be out of loyalty to him. Instead, it will be because she cannot get to her lovers. So, for her relentlessly stubborn refusal to recognize her husband's claims upon her (v. 10), Gomer must be punished (vv. 11-15). After enumerating all that he has provided for Gomer, Hosea then threatens to take it all back from her, leaving her naked and empty.

In the third and last set of threats (vv. 11-15), the husband and the deity have virtually become one. This time it will not be the wife who has the last word (vv. 7,9,14) but the deity/husband (vv. 15,18,19). There is still an echo of Hosea's own voice when he threatens to humiliate her by taking back (*hissaltî*) the fabric that he has provided, and thereby exposing (*ʾăgalleh*) not only her private parts (*nablūtāh*) but her foolishness before her lovers.[18] Precisely here in this threat do the

---

[17] Examples of the growing body of literature on this topic can be seen in works by, Gracia Fay Ellwood, T. Drorah Setel, Judith Ochshorn (especially chap. 3, "Biblical Attitudes Toward Gender"), and Phyllis Trible. The latter does an excellent job in describing what appears to be a common convention among biblical authors and that is the literary expediency of physically victimized women for the sake of the androcentric interests of the biblical narrative.

[18] This is the only occurrence of this form of *nbl* in the Hebrew Bible. Andersen/Freedman correctly point out that the root does not necessarily carry any sexual connotations (Josh. 7:15; I Sam. 25:25; Isa. 9:16; 32:6), although there are clear cases where it does (Judg. 19:23; II Sam. 13:12) especially with the implication of sexual deviation (Andersen/Freedman, 248). This is most likely an example where the prophet/poet is being deliberately ambiguous, where both the wife's genitals and her base, foolish ways are referred to. On the basis of parallelism with 2:11d (*ʿerwātāh*), there is ground to inter-

metaphor and the historical situation of eighth century Israel ingeniously come together and climax. It resounds with Hosea's personal indictment against his wife who is guilty of both brazenly adorning herself with jewelry *(nizmāh wĕḥelyātāh)* that professes her loyalty to others and ascribing to her lovers what he alone has provided her. And it resounds with YHWH's judgment against Israel who is guilty of openly, shamelessly taking part in foreign religious cults (vv. 13-15) and ascribing to other gods *(mĕʿahăbay)* what YHWH alone has done for Israel. Not only will she be exposed, but her merriment brought to an end (vv. 14-15). Despite the harsh tone of judgment that pervades throughout, YHWH/Hosea end their accusations with climactic self-pity, *wĕʾōtî šokhā(h)*, "But me she forgot" (v. 15).

Thus, we discover upon closer examination of the second chapter of Hosea that Hosea and Gomer's marriage was not as harmonious as chaps. 1 and 3 would lead us to believe. In fact, the threats and accusations of 2:4-15 show us the violent, highly erratic side of the otherwise obedient prophet of the other two chapters. Of course, we also discover the stubborn recalcitrant side of the woman Gomer.

The poem concludes, however, on a note of reconciliation (vv. 16-25). In the fourth and fifth strophes, where the speakers switch back and forth between YHWH and Hosea without easy distinction, the mood of the poem has changed drastically. The same amount of pathos that went into threatening Gomer is now spent in seducing her *hinnēh ʾānōkî mĕpateyhā*. Hosea's only desire is to win his wife back. Having been convinced through moral suasion, reasoning, physical punishment, and finally seduction of her husband's claim upon her,[19] Gomer, Hosea imagines, will renounce her former lovers and return to him and never again utter her lovers' names from her lips (v. 19). Convinced of their eventual reconciliation, he envisions the time when she will recognize him for and call him who he truly is: *ʾîšî*. At that time not only will she no longer confuse her husband with other men, neither will she speak the names of her former lovers. Thus, inasmuch as it is her words that help condemn her (vv. 7,9,14), it will be her words that will reconcile her to her husband (vv. 18, 19,25).

From beginning to end, therefore, Hosea is obsessed with persuading Gomer to abandon her lovers and convincing her to acknowledge him as

---

pret *(nablūtāh)* as a direct reference to the woman's sexual parts *(contra* Andersen/Freedman, 248).

[19] Echoing this point, Hans W. Wolff writes, "At first, people are summoned against people; reason is called out against folly, integrity against unfaithfulness ... Thus we have the announcement of at least three different ways in which Yahweh proceeds: (1) he admonishes Israel to turn voluntarily from her pagan gods; (2) he threatens destruction of all possibilities for pagan worship in Palestine; and (3) after leading Israel away from the land, he courts Israel with loving words and acts that represent the eschatological, new beginning of Israel's history" (44).

the provider he is. To be sure, he does not want to kill his wife, though, according to Deuteronomy 22:22 it is his prerogative as a wronged husband to do so. Nor does he wish to humiliate her, but he will if he must. He will do what he must in order to convince her of the folly of her ways. We observe his pain, anguish, uncertainty, anger, and determination to win back his wife. But it appears that Hosea's success in winning Gomer back, however, depends not on the strength of his argument, but the strength of his might.

Hence, sexual violence functions in three ways in this poem.

First, the measures that Hosea takes are expected to demonstrate the extent to which Hosea the betrayed husband will go to preserve his marriage. For example, in v. 8 there is the scene of his futilely trying to block her way with thorns and hem her in with a wall in order to keep her from her lovers and presumably unto himself. She is not a prostitute such that men seek her out, but a wife who pursues men on her own. Therefore, he takes every measure to barricade her in. Moreover, although he has been betrayed he does not take advantage of the two options that were legally his: divorce[20] her or stone her to death.[21] Instead he devises a way to show up her lovers for the frauds they are. Stripping her naked before her lovers will not only expose her body and the foolishness of her ways, it will also prove, contrary to her claims, how feeble and impotent are her lovers to protect and provide for her (v. 12). In a sense, therefore, Gomer becomes a pawn in a match between Hosea (YHWH) and her lovers (other gods), where the aim is to win the loyalty and reverence of the sexually victimized woman. Hosea, the one who has been betrayed, is willing to go to great extremes, even if it means humiliating his wife, in order to win his wife from her lovers.[22]

Sexual violence in 2:4-25 functions secondly to underscore the point that punishment precedes reconciliation. In fact, there is a sense in this poem in which punishment is understood as unavoidable, that punish-

---

[20]Some scholars (e.g., Wolff, 33) have interpreted 2:4 (kî hî' lō' 'ištî wĕ'ānōkî lō' 'îsāh) as a divorce formula. But it is not likely that we should view this statement as a formal divorce decree, especially in light of the fact that the presumption behind the husband's ensuing demands, threats, pleas, and seduction is that he continued to have legal claims upon his wife.

[21]See Deut 22:22. The reference in 2:5 to killing the woman with thirst, according to Andersen/Freedman, is not juridical but historical (222).

[22]It is interesting to note that specific mention of love does not appear in this poem, nor in the entire chapter. Not until we come to the next chapter (3:1) and following, do we find specific mention of the word. Its absence prior to chap. 3 is odd given the extremely emotional nature of and the sensual language found within chap. 2. What is clear, however, is that it is not simply his wife/Israel's love for which the husband/YHWH contends; rather it is his love for her that he seeks to demonstrate (3:1: lēk 'ĕhab 'iššā(h) 'ăhūbt rēa' ûmĕnā'āpet kĕ'ahăbat yĕhwāh 'et bĕnê yiśrā'ēl), albeit in a strange fashion. William Moran contrasts Hosea's preaching on YHWH's love for Israel with that of the Deuteronomist's teaching on Israel's love for YHWH.

ment must be meted out before there can be any possibility of reconciliation. Punishment was within the options of the covenant (Exod 34:6-7; Lev 26; Deut 28), as certainly as death was the fate for an adulterous wife (Deut 22:22). But repeatedly we find YHWH agonizing (2:4; 6:4; 11:8; 13:4) over what is in fact inevitable, non-negotiable, imperative: divine retribution. If punishment were not understood as necessary, there would be no basis for the unrelenting tone of anguish on YHWH's part that pervades the book—nor would there be reason for Hosea's pleading tone with Gomer. To be sure, YHWH's anguish has to do with YHWH's profound disappointment in Israel; but YHWH is also ambivalent about what should be done with Israel. Though it is within YHWH's right to punish Israel, YHWH's love for Israel makes it a difficult task to execute.[23]

Third, and most significant, sexual violence functions as a poetic device to relate the punishment to the crime.[24] It is worth noting that the first formal complaint Hosea registers against Gomer centers around her physical appearance (v. 4). He claims that she brazenly adorns herself with vulgar ornaments that flaunt her infidelity and wantonness. What exactly were zĕnûneyhā and na'ăpûpeyhā, things evidently worn about the face and between the breasts, respectively, remains unclear to the modern reader; they were undoubtedly familiar to Hosea's audience. Whatever they were, Hosea alludes to them and comments on other indecent jewelry in the final complaint in v. 15 where he refers to Gomer decking herself with ring and jewelry before going after her lovers.

Having brought up the image of her illicit apparel early in the poem (v. 4), Hosea immediately proceeds to threaten to strip her, not just of the telltale signs of her unfaithfulness, but strip her "as the day she was born" (v. 5). In v. 11 he refers to the fabric (wool and flax) that he has provided that drapes and covers his wife's body. He threatens to take them back (vv. 11-12). Again the image is of stripping off her garments, exposing her body—not just uncovering her face or her breasts—but undressing her until she is stark naked. One cannot help but wonder if the implication is that had Gomer only taken off the brazen apparel as Hosea had first ordered, she could have been spared public stripping and humiliation. *In other words, the punishment (public stripping) fits the crime (vulgar apparel).*

---

[23] Andersen/Freedman (589). There is no evidence that the abrupt mood change from anguish and threats (2:4-15) to seduction in 2:15f. is because of a change in Gomer/Israel's behavior.

[24] Patrick Miller provides a helpful discussion on the literary motif of correspondence between sin and judgment in prophetic speech.

Attention to the details of the marriage metaphor in Hos 2:4-25, therefore, shows the versatility of the metaphor as a model[25] for shedding light on the capriciousness of the divine-human relationship. One important advantage of this metaphor is its ability to capture the vicissitudes of that relationship. It points out its movement from covenant (marriage) to apostasy (adultery) to punishment/judgment (sexual violence) to covenant renewal (reconciliation). To do that it makes particular use of a range of female sexual experiences such as marriage and adultery, female anatomy and procreation, sexual violence and seduction to call attention to YHWH's faithfulness and Israel's unfaithfulness. Thus, the metaphor provides a wide range of insight into YHWH and Israel's relationship in ways other metaphors cannot. Unlike metaphors which use animal (e.g., heifer, lion, vulture) or inanimate (e.g., morning dew, moth, grapes) images to illustrate such things as YHWH's judgment against Israel or Israel's dependence upon YHWH, the marriage metaphor enables the reader to recognize the more passionate and compassionate side of YHWH. By using the marriage metaphor, Hosea advocated for a relationship between YHWH and people built not simply on absolute obedience and loyalty, but intimacy[26] and (mutual) love. (This was a bold innovation in Ancient Near Eastern religions.) The only other Hoseanic metaphor that begins to match the pathos of the marriage metaphor is the parent-son metaphor found in 11:1f. Despite the intense emotional feelings that pervade 11:1f., the parent-son metaphor was conceived with quasi-political overtones. According to Dennis McCarthy (145), this latter metaphor is concerned with "a love which is seen in reverential fear, in loyalty, and in obedience—a love which can be commanded."[27] The same covenantal notions of reverence and fear, loyalty and obedience undeniably apply in the marriage metaphor.[28] Although marriage in

---

[25]". . . a model is [a] dominant metaphor, a metaphor with staying power . . . some metaphors gain wide appeal and become major ways of structuring and ordering experience," writes Sallie McFague (23).

[26]The kind of intimacy spoken of here is reflected in the word yādēʿāh "know" in 2:10 (daʿat ʾĕlōhîm [4:1;6:6]; haddaʿat [4:6]). It means more than simply intellectual knowledge but the kind of knowledge that comes only from personal intimate interaction. Precisely this kind of knowledge is what YHWH in 2:15 longs for and finds missing in Israel. Such use of yādaʿ carries strong sexual overtones such as found throughout the Hebrew Bible, beginning with Gen. 4:1. Herbert Huffmon has shown that the word is also commonly associated with ancient treaty formulations.

[27]It is interesting to note that although commentators assume it to be the case, there is nothing in the language to suggest that the prophet had in mind the deity as *father* in Hosea 11. In fact, a strong case can be made that the description in 11:1-3 of the deity carrying the young son (Israel) in its arms and teaching young Israel to walk evokes easily the image of YHWH the mother rather than the father.

[28]Along with the article by Gary Hall, Dennis McCarthy's discussion of the close relationship between the marriage motif and the ancient Hebrew concept of covenant is insightful (32).

ancient Israel was more of an economic and social contract than we are accustomed to imagining, judging by the mood of the poem in this study, reverence *and* mutual love, obedience *and* intimacy were not viewed as mutually exclusive elements to be sought in marriage.

Notwithstanding its poetic versatility, nonetheless, elevating the marriage metaphor, or any other metaphor for that matter, to the level of "super model" presents serious problems for biblical and systematic theology. In spite of the fact that it functions as a literary device that draws poetic connections between the nature of Israel's crime and YHWH's punishment, and in spite of its versatility in providing important insights into divine-human relations, how are we as biblical theologians to come to grips with the prophet's association of God with sexual violence? In his sagacious attempt to portray the passionate and compassionate side of YHWH, has the prophet/poet risked those insights when the basic premise of his message evolves around the untenable image of violence against a woman? Does the fact that the marriage metaphor is "*only* a metaphor" and the motif of sexual violence "*only* a theme of the metaphor" insulate them from serious theological scrutiny? While these kinds of questions are beyond the scope of this study, they are not tangential to the exegetical task nor insignificant to biblical scholarship. For in order for the metaphor to make sense, to be exegetically meaningful, the exegete must discern some thread of similarity between the metaphor and the thing signified. Argues Sallie McFague in her fine discussion on this topic in *Metaphorical Theology*, "thinking metaphorically means spotting a thread of similarity between two dissimilar objects, events, or whatever, one of which is better known than the other, and using the better known one as a way of speaking about the lesser known" (15). The problem arises when the metaphor "succeeds," meaning that the reader becomes so engrossed in the pathos and the details of the metaphor that the *dissimilarities* between the two are disregarded. When that happens, McFague points out, God is no longer *like* a husband, God *is* a husband; namely the thing signified *becomes* the signification itself. In this case, a risky metaphor gives rise to a risky deduction: here, to the extent that God's covenant with Israel is like a marriage between a man and a woman, then a husband's physical punishment against his wife is as warranted as God's punishment of Israel. It is the risk of oversimplification and rigid correspondence. It is a risk that we ought always be on guard against. In fact, while the strength of the marriage metaphor is its ability to tell us about YHWH's love, anguish, jealousy, and forgiving nature, it is not capable of shedding any light on the question of divine retribution.[29]

---

[29] The same holds true for questions of power and powerlessness, and sovereignty and dependency.

Analogies have their strengths and their limits. In other words, to the extent that in our modern culture there are no circumstances under which physical punishment is acceptable in marriage, the violent measures Hosea takes to chastise Gomer (should) pose a problem for the modern hearer.

To be sure, these kinds of questions are not novel. They touch upon a larger discussion about religious language and those biblical models that tend to alienate as many people and cultures as they incorporate. For people who know what it is to lose their homeland and be resettled against their will to distant places, the image of God as Commanding Warrior like that found in the conquest narratives (the book of Joshua) may be unacceptable. For societies whose recent history has been marked by the egregious reign of a despot, the image of God as King may be unpalatable. For women who have been the victims of domestic and sexual violence, the image of God as ravaging husband may be intolerable. One thing remains clear: some metaphors—and the marriage metaphor may be one—tend to create more problems than they solve. Therefore, not only is it important, as McFague has urged, to maintain a *diversity* of biblical images and metaphors in order to do justice to "the complexity and richness of the divine-human relationship" (127). *We also must maintain this diversity of metaphors in order to do justice to the richness of human experience.*

Finally, to the extent that religious language and metaphors are not bankrupt as some tend to suppose, that at least in some settings they continue to inspire, mobilize, convict, instruct, challenge, and transform, then the question of the insights and limitations of biblical metaphors should be a priority for all theological enterprises devoted to liberation, especially those who propose to speak for the alienated. Biblical metaphors are not simply examples of grandiloquence, not just instances of literary embellishment where the prophet rather naively or in a moment of inspiration expressed somewhat overdramatically what could have been stated more directly. Instead, they are explicitly what all human language is implicitly, analogical, and therefore limited. Although already doomed to failure, religious language represents human beings' desperate attempts to comprehend and articulate what is in fact beyond comprehension and articulation, the Divine and our experience of it. Biblical metaphors simply heighten our defeat. Biblical metaphors such as one which depends on sexual violence to make its point simply highlight our defeat.

*The writer wishes to thank Dr. Judith Sanderson and her OT60 of Princeton Seminary class whose invitation to lecture on the topic of female sexuality language in the book of Jeremiah provided her with her earliest opportunity to think soberly on the topic.

WORKS CONSULTED

Andersen, F.I. and David N. Freedman
    1980   *Hosea*. AB 24. Garden City: Doubleday.

Alonso-Schokel, Luis
    1960   "Die stilistiche Analyse bein den Propheten." *VTSup* 7: 154-164.
    1975   "Hermeneutical Problems of a Literary Study of the Bible." *VTSup* 28:1-15.
    1983   "Of Methods and Models." *VTSup* 32:3-13.

Buss, Martin
    1969   *The Prophetic Word of Hosea: A Morphological Study*. BZAW 111. Berlin: Topelmann.

Carroll, Robert
    1987   *Jeremiah: A Commentary*. OTL. Philadelphia: Westminster.

Clark, David J.
    1982   "Sex-Related Imagery in the Prophets." *BT* 33:409-13.

Ellwood, Gracia Fay
    1985   "Rape and Judgment." *Daughters of Sarah* 11:9-13.

Exum, J. Cheryl
    1981   "Of Broken Pots, Fluttering Birds and Visions in the Night: Extended Simile and Poetic Technique in Isaiah." *CBQ* 43:331-52.

Fensham, F.C.
    1964-65   "The Covenant-Idea in the Book of Hosea." *OTWSA* 7/8:35-49.

Friedman, Mordechai
    1980   "Israel's Response in Hosea 2:17b: 'You are My Husband'." *JBL* 99:199-204.

Good, Edwin
    1966   "The Composition of Hosea." *SEÅ* 31:21-63.

Guillame, A.
    1964   "A Note on Hosea 2:23,24." *JTS* 15:57-58.

Hall, Gary
    1982   "Origin of the Marriage Metaphor." *Hebrew Studies* 23:169-171.

Huffmon, Herbert B.
    1966   "The Treaty Background of the Hebrew Yādaʿ." *BASOR* 181:31-37.

Huffmon, Herbert B. and Simon B. Parker
    1966   "A Further Note on the Treaty Background of Hebrew Yādaʿ "*BASOR* 184:36-38.

Krszyna, Henryk
    1968   "Literarische Struktur von Os 2:4-17." *BZ* 12:41-59.

McCarthy, Dennis
    1965   "Notes on the Love of God in Deuteronomy and the Father-Son Relationship Between Yahweh and Israel." *CBQ* 27:144-147.
    1972   *Old Testament Covenant*. Oxford: Basil Blackwell.

McFague, Sallie
    1982   *Metaphorical Theology*. Philadelphia: Fortress.

May, Herbert G.
    1932   "The Fertility Cult in Hosea." *AJSL* 48:73-98.

Mays, James
    1969   *Hosea*. Old Testament Library. Philadelphia: Westminster.

Miller, Patrick D.
    1982   *Sin and Judgment in the Prophets*. SBL MS 27. Chico, CA: Scholars Press.

Moran, William
    1963   "The Ancient Near Eastern Background of the Love of God in Deuteronomy." *CBQ* 25:77-87.

Muilenberg, James
    1969   "Form Criticism and Beyond." *JBL* 88:1-18.

Muntingh, L.M.
    1964-5   "Married Life in Israel According to the Book of Hosea." *OTWSA* 7/8:77-84.

Ochshorn, Judith
1981 *The Female Experience and the Nature of the Divine.* Bloomington: Indiana University Press.

Rowley, H.H.
1963 "The Marriage of Hosea." Pp. 66-99 in *Men of God: Studies in Old Testament History and Prophecy.* London: Thomas Nelson.

Rudolph, Wilhelm
1966 *Hosea.* KAT 13/1. Gutersloh: Gerd Mohn.

Setel, T. Drorah
1985 "Prophets and Pornography: Female Sexual Imagery in Hosea." Pp. 86-95 in *Feminist Interpretation of the Bible.* Ed. Letty Russell. Philadelphia: Westminster.

Trible, Phyllis
1984 *Texts of Terror.* Philadelphia: Fortress.

Vogels, W.
1981 "'Osée-Gomer' car et comme 'Yahweh-Israel' Os 1-3." *NRTh* 103:711-727.

Weinfeld, Moshe
1972 *Deuteronomy and the Deuteronomic School.* Oxford: Oxford University Press.

Willis, John T.
1985 "Dialogue Between Prophet and Audience as a Rhetorical Device in the Book of Jeremiah." *JSOT* 33:63-82.

Wolff, Hans W.
1974 *Hosea.* Hermeneia. Trans. Gary Stansell. Philadelphia: Fortress.

A CHAMBERLAIN'S JOURNEY AND THE CHALLENGE OF INTERPRETATION FOR LIBERATION

Clarice J. Martin
Princeton Theological Seminary

ABSTRACT

A survey of the literature on the Ethiopian eunuch's conversion in Acts 8:26-40 reveals a predominant interest in its prophecy-fulfillment character and apologetic tenor. The Ethiopian's ethnographic identity and geographic provenance have, by contrast, received negligible attention. In fact, his ethnographic identity in particular has been characterized as both "indeterminable" and "inconsequential" for Luke's theological purposes in Acts. These theses have been roundly challenged in this essay, with the methodological issues engendered by a "hermeneutics of suspicion" receiving particular analysis. An introductory review of (1) some of the theological trajectories of the pericope is followed by (2) a documentary assessment of the Ethiopian's ethnographic identity, (3) his geographic provenance, and finally (4) an analysis of the impact of how a "politics of omission" has been operative in perpetuating a lack of familiarity with Ethiopians in antiquity and in contemporary culture.

Edward J. Young has aptly described the story of the Ethiopian treasurer in Acts 8:26-40 as "one of the most beautiful incidents recorded in the book of Acts" (132). Also described as a "diamond in the rough whose brilliance can be detected only after close examination," (Karris, 1978:99), this *resplendissant et pittoresque tableau* of a peregrinating Ethiopian high official has long been the object of both fascination and curiosity.

Ernest Haenchen calls the inquisitive traveler a "chamberlain," an honorific though pristine epithet for the treasurer of Queen Candace (309). The term "chamberlain," derived from the Old French "chamberlenc," identifies one who is either (1) an attendant on a royal or noble chamber (usually a large room with a vaulted roof), or (2) a steward of a king or queen (Hoad, 69-70; Partridge, 72-73). The latter definition is most appropriate for the Ethiopian official in Acts 8:26-40.

The story of the Ethiopian's conversion has received scant attention in the history of the twentieth century scholarly biblical research. The dearth of material is immediately apparent when works on the subject are examined. In 1911 E.C. Selwyn wrote a brief exegetical study of Acts 8:26-40 (273-84). François Bovon cites only one study of the pericope in his *Luc le theologien: Vinqt-cinq ans de recherches (1950-1975)* (Bovon), and the solitary article listed by Bovon is only five pages in length (Squillaci).

More recent publications offer insightful discussions of the pericope, usually in conjunction with other leading interests, but the number of these articles is negligible (e.g., Brodie, Grassi, Lindijer, O'Toole, Mínguez). The recent full-scale study of Acts 8:26-40 by William Frank Lawrence is a welcome addition to the literature (Lawrence), and this writer's own study may shed additional light on the complexities of the pericope (Martin).

This brief review of some of the extant studies of Acts 8:26-40 shows why the eager researcher often meets with disappointing results in the search for extensive and detailed studies of the pericope. Commentaries on the book of Acts provide some consolation in this quest; however, the harvest is generally meager here as well.[1]

Corresponding to the issue of the dearth of studies on the pericope is the issue of the normative ideological and theological focus of the pericope. Most studies identify familiar--though important--theological trajectories of the story, but neglect or deemphasize other aspects, such as the potential signification of an Ethiopian high official for the Lucan perspective. This article will review and highlight some of the "familiar" trajectories, and explore in more detail some of its neglected aspects.

The Ethiopian's Conversion: Theological Trajectories

Traditional exegetical studies of Acts 8:26-40 have brought to light several illuminating theological trajectories which echo recurrent Lucan motifs elsewhere in Luke-Acts.

First, the numerous allusions to the action of the Holy Spirit throughout the story (Acts 8:26, 29, 39)[2] recall the Lucan emphasis on

---

[1] But cf. Haenchen (309-17), Bruce (1984:198-96), and Marshall (1983: 160-66), *inter alia*.

[2] The phrase "angel of the Lord" appears to be interchangeable with "Spirit of the Lord," denoting the "agency of the divine presence of God" (Bruce, 1984:141, 190). Williams calls both terms "synonyms" for God's acts of self-revelation (119). Haenchen notes that the only other story so distinguished by divine intervention determining the

the strategic role of the Holy Spirit in preaching and evangelism (Lk. 4:18; 24:44; Acts 1:8; 4:8-10; 7:55; 10:11-12; 13:4-10; 16:6-7).

Second, Philip's preaching to the Ethiopian highlights a second recurrent Lucan theme: the "witness" motif. The strategic role of the early Christians' witness to the significance of the events of Jesus' life, death, and resurrection (Lk. 1:1-4; 24:48; Acts 1:21-22; 4:33; 10:39-41; 22:14-15) is here illustrated again.

Third, the response of the Ethiopian to the conversion experience itself, in which we see him "going home rejoicing," recalls the abundant terminological expressions for "joy" in the Lucan writings (Lk. 1:44; 2:10; 15:4-7; 19:6, 37; 24:41; Acts 2:47; 8:8; 11:18; 16:33).

Chief among the Lucan theological motifs and interests in Acts 8:26-40 is a "prophecy-fulfillment" or "proof-from-prophecy" pattern which is acknowledged to be especially characteristic of the Lucan writings.[3] "Prophecy-fulfillment" here means the fulfillment of the Old Testament (promise, prophecy, etc.) in such a way as to establish historical continuity between Israel and the church (Talbert, 92). But in agreement with Talbert's thesis, the definition is broader than this, and includes the fulfillment of prophetic utterances or promises within the New Testament itself, as in prophetic statements uttered by the risen Christ regarding the evangelistic outreach of the church which are fulfilled (94).

For Luke, Isaiah 53:7ff. exemplifies such a prophecy-fulfillment function, and becomes the *locus classicus* for preaching Jesus (euēggelisato autǫ tov Iēsouv) in Acts 8:26-40.[4] It is in response to the Ethiopian's inquisitive and unrelenting desire to know "about whom the prophet speaketh" that Philip the Evangelist, "beginning with this scripture" (arxamenos apo tēs graphēs tautēs) launches into his exposition of the "good news of Jesus."[5] Edward J. Young underscores the centrality and importance of the apologetic use of Isaiah 53:7ff. in the narrative development when he describes the Isaiah passage as providing "privileged" opportunities for the *dramatis personae* to both "preach" and "hear" its explication (with reference to the life of Jesus):

---

course of events in Acts "at every turn" is the Cornelius story (315). For other examples of similar divine directives in Acts, cf. Acts 10:19; 13:2; 16:6f.

[3] For discussions of this schema in the literature, cf. Lohse, Dupont (1953b), Tiede, Karris (1979), Schubert, Kurz (1976), and Dahl (1980).

[4] Acts 8:35. The larger passage from which the Old Testament citation is taken is Isaiah 52:13-53:12, the last and most well-known of the Servant songs. As C.H. Dodd observed, parts of this last song are represented in one way or another in almost every part of the New Testament (92-94). Allusions to this Servant song are also found in the Synoptic gospels, John, Acts, Hebrews and 1 Peter.

[5] The phrase "the good news of Jesus" is the rendering of "euēggelisato" in the Revised Standard Version of the New Oxford Annotated bible, which is used throughout this essay unless otherwise indicated (May and Metzger).

> To this eunuch fell the privilege of asking--and it is the first recorded instance of the question being asked--of whom the prophet in the fifty-third chapter of Isaiah was speaking. And to Philip was granted the privilege of giving a definite answer to the eunuch's question (132).

Luke's colorful depiction of Philip's exposition of the Isaiah 53 passage indicates that already within the church there was an understanding of the Suffering Servant passages as fulfilled in Christ (Dodd: 132). Barnabas Lindars has suggested that Isaiah 53:7ff. was used with other Old Testament passages in the early preaching primarily for apologetic purposes, with Luke here drawing upon the stock of apologetic biblical material to illustrate how the mission of the Servant had been achieved in Jesus' death and resurrection. The particular value of Isaiah 53 for the early church is its revelation of a predetermined divine plan that the Messiah should suffer: "Jesus suffered because he is the Christ, and the Christ must suffer" (77).

Luke uses the Old Testament to confirm the fulfillment of God's promise in three additional ways. First, the conversion of the Ethiopian eunuch qua "eunuch" (eunouchos) represents the fulfillment of Isaiah 56:3-7, which heralds a day when eunuchs will be accepted into the assembly of the Lord. As early as 1920, Alfred Loisy proposed that Luke "invented" the pericope to represent the fulfillment of this Old Testament citation (62).

Isaiah 56:3-7 contains a promise that the old regulation in Deut. 23:1 forbidding the entrance of eunuchs into the assembly of God will be abolished:

> [3] Let not the foreigner who has joined himself to the Lord say, "The Lord will surely separate me from his people"; and let not the eunuch say, "Behold I am a dry tree."
> [4] For thus says the Lord: "To the eunuchs who keep my sabbaths, who choose the things that please me and hold fast my covenant,
> [5] I will give in my house and within my walls a monument and a name better than sons and daughters; I will give them an everlasting name which shall not be cut off.
> [6] "And the foreigners who join themselves to the Lord, to minister to him, to love the name of the Lord, and to be his servants, every one who keeps the sabbath, and does not profane it, and holds fast my covenant--
> [7] these I will bring to my holy mountain, and make them joyful in my house of prayer; their burnt offerings and their sac-

rifices will be accepted on my altar; for my house shall be called a house of prayer for all peoples."

Isaiah 56:3-7 anticipates a time of "full class membership" for eunuchs--a move from communal isolation and marginality to communal inclusion and wholeness.[6] For Luke, the conversion of the Ethiopian eunuch represents the realization of this vision. C.S.C. Williams argues that the Ethiopian eunuch's conversion qua "eunuch" is, in fact, the chief reason for its inclusion in the story, for Luke's main purpose is to show that "the Gospel was taken not only to the half-caste Samaritans but even to one who because he was a eunuch could never have belonged to the Old Israel (118-19)."

Second, the Ethiopian's conversion exhibits the fulfillment of the promise of an unconditional and prodigious acceptance of foreigners (ho allogenēs)[7] into the community in accordance with Isaiah 56:3-7.[8] The Ethiopian becomes a prototype of the "foreigner" who enjoys unconditional acceptance into the new eschatological community. Finally, the conversion of the Ethiopian eunuch demonstrates the fulfillment of the prophecy in Psalm 68:31 that Ethiopia will "stretch out her hands to God;"[9]

---

[6] According to Claus Westermann, the new conditions in Isaiah 56:3-8 indicate that the old concept of the chosen people is here giving way to "a new order of things," where acting righteously and keeping the sabbath are the grounds for participation in the community. "As early as here we find present important elements of the New Testament's concept of community (169)."

[7] The translation is taken from Joseph Ziegler, ed., *Isaias* (56).

[8] The Ethiopian was a Nubian from Meroë. His ethnographic identity will receive further discussion in this essay under "The Ethiopian's Identity: Its Ethnographic Significance." That the Ethiopian eunuch was a Gentile is widely admitted, although with some dissent. Loisy called him "le premier les païens dans la communauteé." Martin Dibelius and Etienne Trocmé identify him as a "God-fearing Gentile" (phoboumenos ton theon)--a designation applied to Cornelius in Acts 10:2. But cf. Haenchen, who argues that Luke leaves the Ethiopian's religious status "in doubt" "because he would have forestalled the Gentile mission." See: Loisy (3810, Dibelius (121), Trocmé (314).

[9] Psalm 68:31 is but one of many Old Testament citations which refer to Ethiopia. Cf. Esther 1:1; Job 28:19; Isaiah 11:11; 18:1--2; 20:3-5; 37:9; Jer 13:23; 38:7-13; Ezek. 29:10; Amos 9:7; Nahum 3:9. Edward Ullendorf confirms that Ethiopia (Aithiopia) is rendered "Cush" by the LXX, and that it is generally used to refer to the entire Nile Valley south of Egypt including both Nubia and Abyssinia (5).

Psalm 68:31 is "undoubtedly" the favorite Bible quotation in modern Ethiopia, occurring twice in the *Kebra Nagast* (the repository of Ethiopian national and religious teachings) and used frequently as a motto. "Ethiopia 'stretching out her hands to God' has become a proof-text and symbol of the country's orthodox faith." (Ullendorf 9).

The Greek and Ethiopic texts of Psalm 68:31 are clear, but the Hebrew contains some textual problems, particularly the sense of yadayw. An alternative to the RSV translation cited above has been proposed by Mitchell Dahood and others. Dahood suggests that the sense of yadayw, "his hands," seems to connote "the product of his hands, his wares." The translation would then be: "Let Ethiopia bring her possessions to God." A.A. Anderson proposes that this translation would give a reasonable parallel to 68:31a. This sense is preserved by Roland Murphy: "Gifts are to be brought to Yahweh in Jerusalem from the

> Let bronze be brought from Egypt, let Ethiopia hasten
> to stretch out her hands to God.

Appropriately, in Acts 8:26-40, Luke portrays just such an eager reconnoiter in the figure of the Ethiopian treasurer.

The Ethiopian's Identity: Its Ethnographic Significance

If a provocative mosaic of the theological character of Acts 8:26-40 can be readily ascertained through an analysis of exegetical notations from commentaries, articles and monographs on the subject, the ethnographic identity of one of the leading protagonists in the story--the Ethiopian eunuch--is virtually ignored. And when the ethnographic identity of the Ethiopian is admitted explicitly as that of a recognizable black African from ancient Nubia, development of the significance of this data for the Lucan theological perspective is rarely attempted. In short, examination of the Ethiopian's ethnographic identity is generally perceived to be *non est tanti*.

A survey of the literature reveals at least three approaches to the Ethiopian's ethnographic identity. The first is "uncertainty." F.D. Gealy argues that Luke avoids the matter altogether. While admitting that he is an "Ethiopian" and an "outlander," Gealy nevertheless concludes: "*his ethnic origin is strictly undetermined* (177-78, italics mine).

Within the context of this prevailing uncertainty, Nils Dahl especially cautions the reader against concluding that the Ethiopian is black. Further, and most importantly--he concludes that the Ethiopian's nationality is of no consequence:

> What made his conversion to be remembered and told as a legend was neither his African provenance nor his black skin. *(It is quite possible that he was black, but that is never said . . .).* In the Lucan composition his story has been placed between the evangelization among the Samaritans and the vocation of Paul, preparing for the mission to the Gentiles. Thus we get a picture of a progressive widening of the circle reached by the gospel; *but the question of nationality has no special importance* (Dahl, 1974:62-63. italics mine).

'nations' . . . This hymn urges 'kingdoms' to acknowledge Yahweh, enthroned in his sanctuary.'" See Dahood (151), Anderson (498), and Murphy (588).

With a second and common approach to the Ethiopian's ethnographic identity, his place of origin, Nubia, is admitted, but usually with only a cursory discussion of Nubia, and rarely with any explicit identification of Nubians (or "Ethiopians" as they were called in the Common Era) as black-skinned people (e.g., Dupont, 1953a; Haenchen; Foakes-Jackson; Marshall, 1983; Munck; Rackham).

With the third approach, the reader is more clearly and explicitly apprised of the ethnographic identity of an "Ethiopian" eunuch in the Lucan narrative. Writing as early as 1922, Theodor Zahn described him as "ein Äïthiope" from a region bordering on the Egyptian Nile and inhabited by "mehr oder weniger negerartigen Volksstämmen" (311).

The glaring lack of concrete descriptive detail regarding the Ethiopian's identity in Acts 8:26-40 is surprising in view of the prodigious classical evidence. The word for Ethiopian, "Aethiops," a derivative of the Greek Aithiops, was the most common generic word denoting a Negroid type in Greco-Roman usage. A summary of Greek and Roman anthropological observations preserved in classical literature identifies Ethiopians as dark-skinned; in fact, as Snowden observes, "skin color was uppermost in the minds of the Greeks and Romans, whether they were describing Ethiopians in the land of their origin or their expatriated congeners in Egypt, Greece, or Italy" (1979:2). Snowden's graphic description of the significance of the Ethiopian's appearance in the Greco-Roman world is worth noting here:

> Blackness and the Ethiopian were . . . in many respects synonymous . . . The Ethiopians' blackness became proverbial, and gave rise to the expression Aîthîopa smēcheiv, "to wash an Ethiopian white." . . . *Ethiopians were the yardstick by which antiquity measured colored peoples.* The skin of the Ethiopian was black, in fact, blacker, it was noted, than that of any other people. Indians were dark or black--the Indians whom Alexander visited were said to be blacker than the rest of mankind with the exception of Ethiopians (1979:5, 23, italics mine).

While the distinguishing mark of the Ethiopian was the color of his skin, several other characteristics were persistently applied to Ethiopians: "puffy" or "thick" lips, tightly curled or "wooly" hair, a flat or "broad" nose. In fact, as G.H. Beardsley observes, the extensive appearance of blacks in sixth century Greek art was directly related to their memorable appearance--their characteristically "wooly" hair and "large everted lips" on vases and other art mediums "leaves no doubt that they served as models for the potter" (11-12).

In fact, one of the greatest witnesses of Africa migration northward to Egypt, Greece, and Italy is provided by classical art. From the sixth century onward artists have used the black as a model in almost every medium, and "as a favorite in many" (Snowden, 1979:23). Greek and Roman artists exhibited an incomparable and "continuous interest" in the Ethiopian, rendering the black with the "utmost fidelity," even during the most restrained and idealistic period of Greek art (Beardsley, ix, x). The popular depiction of the black in Greco-Roman art is corroborated by massive artistic evidence in stone, iron, marble, bronze, terra cotta and plastic. Negro images appeared on jewelry, tombs, shields, coins, pelikes, skypos, askos, lekythos, head-vases, busts, statues, and masks, and represented a wide range of occupational and other socio-cultural involvements in Greece and Rome.[10]

By the first century of the Common Era the term "Ethiopia" was used especially of the kingdom of Meroë, the seat of government in Nubia. Located between the 5th and 6th cataracts, Meroë became the capital city of the region in about 540 B.C.E., when the royal family relocated there from Napata. Its strategic location near the Nile River proved advantageous for preserving the generally fertile, cultivable land used for crops and herds, and for facilitating travel for caravans traveling east and west.[11] Torgny Säve-Soderbergh's description of

---

[10] Beardsley notes that the "Negro type" in classical art is so common that a complete list is difficult to amass (x). Her study, *The Negro in Greek and Roman Civilization*, contains illuminating and striking images dating from the fifth century B.C.: cf. Fig. 20, a bronze Ethiopian boy, possibly a musician, p. 98, Hellenistic period; Fig. 21, the conjoined heads in a tricephalic agate, with an Ethiopian woman who may be connected with the ruling family of Meroë, p. 109.

Also useful are the artistic depictions (often in color) found in Frank Snowden, Jr., "Iconographical Evidence on the Black Populations in Greco-Roman Antiquity," *The Image of the Black in Western Art. From the Pharaoh to the Fall of the Roman Empire* (Snowden, 1976:133-245), and Jehan Desanges, "The Iconography of the Black in Ancient North Africa," *The Image of the Black in Western Art. From the Pharaohs to the Fall of the Roman Empire* (246-68). For other artistic renditions, cf. the work by Mary B. Comstock and Cornelius C. Vermule, *Sculpture in Stone: The Greek, Roman and Etruscan Collections of the Museum of Fine Arts, Boston* (Comstock and Vermule), which includes a striking figure entitled: "Negro Boy Seated," either a captive or genre study on an Alexandrian or Corinthian Street, 100 B.C.-100 A.D., Fig. 112; and David Finn and Caroline Houser, *Greek Monumental Bronze Sculpture* (Finn and Houser), who provide an illustrative depiction of the bronze "Negro Boy Jockey and Horse," ca. 2-3 century B.C., Pompeii.

[11] The history of ancient Nubia is divided into three major periods: the Napatan (751-542 B.C.) when Napata was the seat of government, the Meroitic (542 B.C.-339/350 A.D.), when Meroë became the seat of government, and the X-Group period (339/350–550 A.D.). For a helpful introductory survey of the history of ancient Nubia cf.: Margaret Shinnie, *Ancient African Kingdoms* (Shinnie); and works by William Y. Adams: *Nubia: Corridor to Africa* (Adams, 1977); "Post-Pharonic Nubia in the Light of Archaeology, I," (Adams, 1964); and "Post-Pharaonic Nubia in the Light of Archaeology, II," (Adams, 1965).

Nubia as the "Corridor of Africa" is no misnomer for this meeting place of cultures between the Mediterranean world and Africa (20).

Ethiopian involvement in the Greco-Roman world predates the sixth century B.C.E. Greek (Ionian and Carian) mercenaries served in the Nubian campaigns of Psammetichus I (Psalmlik) in 663-609 B.C.E. Roman contact with Ethiopians in the Imperial period was facilitated by military activity in Egypt--a factor which accounts for the more numerous allusions to Ethiopians in Imperial Rome than Republican Rome (Snowden, 1976). Roman excursions into Meroë have been documented by the geographer Strabo.[12]

Greco-Roman literary evidence for the Ethiopian as a recognizably black African is compelling. Most notable among the earliest numerous allusions to the Ethiopians' appearance is the Homeric description of Eurybates, the herald who attended Odysseus and accompanied him from Ithaca to Troy in the *Odyssey*.

> Furthermore, a herald attended him, a little older than he, and I will tell thee of him too, what manner of man he was. *He was round shouldered, dark of skin, and curly-haired*, and his name was Eurybates; and Odysseus honoured him above his other comrades, because he was like-minded with himself.[13] (italics mine)

The Greek adjective used to describe Eurybates, melanochroos, means "black" (Liddell and Scott: 1095). It was in reply to Penelope's request for a description of the comrades accompanying her husband that the disguised Odysseus mentioned Eurybates--and the mention of Eurybates was one of the sure tokens which Penelope recognized as proof of her husband (Snowden, 1979:102).

The Greek historian Herodotus, writing in the fifth century B.C., records numerous impressions of his visit to Africa, and frequently alludes to Ethiopians.[14] His description of the Ethiopians' hair betrays the perennial interest and familiarity with the appearance of Nubians in antiquity:

> ... but they of Libya have of all men *the wooliest hair*.[15] (Italics mine)

---

[12] Strabo 17.1.54. Horace Leonard Jones, trans. *The Geography of Strabo* (Jones).
[13] Homer, *Odyssey* 19.244.248. A.T. Murray, trans. (1960a).
[14] Herodotus 2.29-32; 3.17-24; 4.183, 197.
[15] Herodotus 7.70.

The Roman Seneca, writing in the Common Era, proposes that the African sun and heat are responsible for the Ethiopian's skin color:

> First of all, the *burnt color of the people* indicates that Ethiopia is very hot...[16] (italics mine)

In a period when it was believed that the climate flora, fauna, and topography influenced the appearance of the human inhabitants of a given region, Seneca's assertion would not be construed as unusual.

With our review of some of the massive classical evidence about the Ethiopian's ethnographic identity the question which must be asked is: What is the significance *for Luke* of the inclusion of a story about a recognizably *black* African official? Since Luke's readers would not have suffered from nebulous illusions about the identity or appearance of Ethiopians, in what way would the inclusion of the story of the conversion of an Ethiopian eunuch *qua* "Ethiopian" eunuch coincide with Luke's general theological concerns (inclusive of the functions cited above under "Theological Trajectories")? We grant, with Haenchen, that the story may represent the first Gentile conversion in Hellenistic circles--a conversion effected by Philip--and perhaps a "rival" or parallel to the story of the first Gentile conversion effected by Peter (315). But is it plausible that, as Dahl argues, that "the question of nationality has no special importance" for Luke (1974:62-63)? The subject deserves careful reexamination.

We would argue that the story of a *black* African Gentile from what would be perceived as a "distant nation" to the south of the empire is consistent with the Lucan emphasis on "universalism," a recurrent motif in both Luke and Acts, and one that is well known.[17] The declaration that the salvation accomplished in Christ is not ethnocentric--but is available to both Jew and Greek,[18] is already heard at the beginning of the Third Gospel ("'All flesh' shall see the salvation of God," Lk. 3:6), with the universal scope of the Christian kerygma given a most forceful and explicit expression at the end of the gospel ("Repentance and forgiveness of sins shall be preached to 'all nations'" Lk. 24:47).

---

[16] Seneca. *Naturales Questiones* IV A. 218. The *fons et origio* of this ancient anthropological formulation of ethnographic differences in humans was Hippocrates. See his *On Airs, Waters, Places* (Snowden, 1979:172).

[17] Cf. John Navone, *Themes of St. Luke* (Navone); Jacob Jervell, "The Divided People of God: The Restoration of Israel and Salvation of the Gentiles" (Jervell); S.G. Wilson, *The Gentiles and the Gentile Mission in Luke-Acts* (Wilson); Robert F. O'Toole, *The Unity of Luke's Theology: An Analysis of Luke-Acts* (O'Toole, 1984).

[18] Although Luke does preserve Israel's prerogative--salvation is to the Jew first, and also to the Greek (Acts 13:46).

Luke's special source "L"[19] reinforces this emphasis of the universal mission of Jesus and the Christian church. The "sign of Jonah" story continues the emphasis on the reception of Jesus by non-Jews (Lk. 11:29-32), as does the story of the centurion of Capernaum (Lk. 7:5), and the story about the Samaritans (17:11-19).

Both Luke and Matthew preserve banquet scene traditions in which the invitation to the eschatological feast is issued to both the original invitees and subsequently, to those "outsiders" in the "thoroughfares and streets" (Mt. 22:9-10), and the "highways and hedges" (Lk. 14:23). We are elsewhere told that those who "sit at table" with Abraham, Isaac and Jacob will come from "east and west" (Mt. 7:8-12 par. Lk. 13:29), but Luke alone here adds "north and south" (cf. Lk. 13:29). Luke's explicit addition is interesting in view of the Ethiopian's provenance, for the Ethiopian's conversion enables the reader to envision proleptically just such an interloper form the "south" in attendance[20] at the eschatological banquet.

Lucan universalism in Acts is also well-documented. In the first chapter in Acts mission to the "end of the earth" is proclaimed. The sense of the eventual geographical expansiveness of the proclamation is evident in the Pentecost story (Acts 2), which has in view "Jews from every nation under heaven," including a specific list of nations represented.[21]

The preaching to the Samaritans (Acts 8:4-8) marks yet another advance to the Gentiles, with the Cornelius story representing for Luke the decisive inauguration of the *Heiden Mission* (Acts 10:1-11:18). The Lucan theme of universal salvation and world mission unfolds throughout Acts as the Gospel advances northward from Palestine through An-

---

[19] As is well known in Synoptic source criticism, "L" refers to traditional material, whether written or oral, peculiar to the Third Gospel. For a helpful survey of the "L" passage see Joseph A. Fitzmyer,*The Gospel According to Luke: A New Translation with Introduction and Commentary* (Fitzmyer, 1981b).

[20] The Lucan addition is interesting in spite of Marshall's observation that "'East and West' together mean the whole world (Mal. 1:11; Zc. 8:7; Is. 59:19)" (Marshall, 1978:568). Fitzmyer argues that the phrase "north and south" should be a part of the original text from which it is taken, Ps. 107:3 (Fitzmyer, 1981b:1026).

[21] There is some question as to whether the "list of nations" is originally Lucan. In 1948 Stefan Weinstock argued that the list of nations, which consists almost exclusively of Near Eastern countries (Western Asia Minor, Northeast Africa) showed striking similarities to the astrological treatise of Paulus Alexandrinus (ca. 4th Century A.D.). Did Paulus and Luke both reproduce an older pre-Christian list? Bruce M. Metzger argues, contra, Weinstock, that many more differences than similarities exist between the two documents. Cf. Stefan Weinstock, "The Geographical Catalogue in Acts II, 9-11, (Weinstock, 44-46); Metzger, "Ancient Astrological Geography in Acts 2:9-11" (Metzger).

For the suggestion of J.A. Brinkman that the literary background of the catalogue is Babylonian-Hellenistic, see Brinkman, "The Literary Background of the 'Catalogue of Nations', Acts 2, 9-11" (Brinkman). For the view that the list is a pre-Lucan Christian missions list see Bo Reicke, "Glaube and Leben der Urgemeinde. Bemerkungen zu Apg. 1-7." (Reicke).

tioch (Acts 9:32-12:24), westward through Asia Minor (12:25-16:5), Europe (Acts 16:6-19:20), and finally to Rome (Acts 19:21-28:310, the "capital" of the Gentile world (Green, 112). Universalism in Luke-Acts underscores the certainty that the mission of Jesus and his church are "united in the plan of God for the salvation of all nations" (Navone, 187). The conversion of an "Ethiopian" eunuch provides a graphic illustration and symbol of the diverse persons who will constitute the Church of the Risen Christ.

In fact, the premise that the Ethiopian represents what Snowden calls "a symbol of the peoples out of whom the Church was destined to grow" (1979:198) has been admitted elsewhere in early Church tradition. Augustine proposes this symbolic function of "Ethiopia" in general in his comments on Psalm 68:31 ("Let bronze be brought from Egypt, let Ethiopia stretch out her hands to God") when he says:

> Under the name of Egypt or of Ethiopia he hath signified the faith of all nations . . . he hath signified the nations of the whole world (Schaff, 298).

According to Jean Marie Courtès, the Augustinian interpretation is an example of "a strong bond . . . between the explication of the faith and the Ethiopian theme . . . intended to extend the promise and possibility of salvation to all of mankind (sic)" (30).

Athanasius also finds "Ethiopians" to be appropriate figures for representing the conversion of all nations. In his *Expositio in Psalmos,* he marvels of Psalm 68:31 that "by 'Kushites' God indicates the end of the earth . . . For how Kush ran to the preaching is possible to see from the believing Ethiopian . . . God shows that all the other nations also believe in Christ with their Kings.[22]

The Ethiopian's Provenance: Its Geographic Significance

The geographic significance of the Ethiopian's conversion is generally designated in missiological terms. Bruce's words are characteristic of this sentiment: "It marks the progress of the Christian mission not only outside Jerusalem, but represents a further advance toward the evangelization of the Gentiles" (Bruce: 1976:190). Johannes Munck also observes that Philip's missionary activity in Judea and Samaria (which includes the encounter with the Ethiopian) initiates mission to the world, effectively "breaking the bar between Israel and the people

---

[22] I am indebted to Courtès for this citation in the Patristic literature (Courtès: 22). For Athansius' translation, see Robert W. Thompson.(108).

outside" (8) and thus sets the stage for the great discussion between the Jerusalem church and the mission churches regarding the admission of Gentiles into the Church (Acts 15). Haenchen calls the conversion of the Ethiopian a "stepping-stone" between the conversion of the Samaritans and the Gentiles which illustrates the progress of the mission (314, 316).

Mentioned less frequently is the significance of the Ethiopian's provenance for Acts 1:8, which many scholars consider to be the "keynote" or "programmatic" focus of the narrative of Acts. Here the Risen Christ declares to his followers:

> But you shall receive power when the Holy Spirit has come upon you, and you shall be my witnesses in Jerusalem and in all Judea and Samaria and to the end of the earth.

The suggestion of this paper is that Acts 1:8c in particular which forecasts mission "to the end of the earth" (eschaton tēs gēs)[23] finds a symbolic--though partial--fulfillment in Acts 8:26-40 when the converted Ethiopian returns home to "Ethiopia" (Nubia), for in ancient geography "Ethiopia" represented "the end of the earth" to the south in the Greco-Roman world.

Proponents of the view that Acts 1:8c is fulfilled in Acts 8:26-40, though few, are explicit in identifying this correspondence. One of the earliest and most detailed observations which link Ethiopians with the "end of the earth" is that of Theodor Zahn, who says of the pericope in general: "Es handelt sich um einem am Ende der damals bekannten Welt (cf. AG 1:8) geborenen Heiden . . ." (312). H.J. Cadbury theorizes that Luke included Acts 8:26-40 "to illustrate the fulfillment of the promise" with which Acts begins of witnessing in Judea and Samaria and to the end of the earth," (1955:15), since "to Homer and to Isaiah the Ethiopians doubtless represented a geographical extreme," the Ethiopian "is certainly a representative of the ends of the earth" (1979:66).

Martin Hengel's most succinct and graphic explication of the correspondence between Acts 1:8c and 8:26-40 is especially helpful:

> As a result of the expulsion of the "Hellenists" from Jerusalem, the gospel was passed on to Samaria and *finally, in the figure of the Ethiopian on his way home, reached the "end of the earth."* (Zeph. 3:10; Ps. 68:32; Lk 11:31) (80, italics mine).

---

[23] There is widespread agreement among New Testament exegetes that Luke derived Acts 1:8c from Isaiah 49:6. For a thorough discussion of the use of the phrase in the LXX see W.C. Van Unnik.

T.C.G. Thornton has written perhaps the sole study of the correspondence between Acts 1:8c and 8:26-40.64. In this brief exposition Thornton effectively challenges the popular thesis that mission to the "end of the earth" is fulfilled solely with Paul's arrival in Rome, the *Endpunkt* of the narrative of Acts (Acts 28:16) (Thornton, 35). In Thornton's words, with the Ethiopian returning home, the Gospel has "already reached the end of the earth, and this end is Ethiopia" (374).

While Zahn, Cadbury, Hengel and Thornton corroborate this correspondence between Acts 1:8c and 8:26-40, their arguments suffer from a lack of specific detail and documentation, and the significance of this geographical data is nowhere elucidated with expansive and critical analysis. The annals of ancient geographical literature in particular-- and other classical literary documents in general--provide formidable support for their identification of Ethiopia as the "end of the earth" to the south. Specific examples of the perception of Ethiopia's geographical location in ancient cosmology are appropriate here.

Greek and Roman writers identified four major groups of peoples who lived toward the edges of the inhabited world: to the north were the "Scythians," to the south the "Ethiopians," to the east were "Indians," and to the west the "Celts" or "Iberians." It should be remembered that these geographical ideas were based primarily on literary and oral traditions rather than scientific investigations (Thornton, 374).

In primitive Homeric geography the earth was a circular plane surrounded on all sides by "Ocean," a continuous circumfluent stream flowing around the earth. Not a "sea" but a mighty river flowing around the earth in which the sun set and rose, Ocean was the parent of all waters, including rivers, seas and fountains (Bunbury, I:34,76). It was believed that Ethiopia bordered on the southern edge of the stream of Ocean, as attested by the *Iliad*. When we read that Iris is going to the land of the Ethiopians "near the Ocean" its significance is immediately apparent:

> I may not sit, for I must go back unto the streams of Oceanus, unto the land of the Ethiopians, where they are sacrificing hecatombs to the immortals, that I too may share in the sacred feast. (Iliad, 23.205-207, Murray, 1960b, italics mine)

Herodotus, writing in the fifth century B.C., traveled extensively, recording his experiences of the ethnographic and geographic diversity of the world as he saw it, and as he heard it from traveler's tales and the experience of explorers. According to John Ball, Herodotus located

Ethiopia to the west of Asia (12). Herodotus described Ethiopia as the most distant country and peoples to the southwest:[24]

> Where the south inclines westwards, the part of the world stretching fartherest toward the sunset is Ethiopia; here is great plenty of gold, and abundance of elephants . . . and the people are the tallest and fairest and longest-lived of all men. *These then are the Libyans* (Herodotus 3.114-15, Godley, italics mine).

Herodotus elsewhere refers to Ethiopians as those who dwell "on the Libyan coast of the southern sea," and he identified Meroë as the "capital of all Ethiopia" (Herodotus 3.17ff., and 3.25ff.).

By the first century of the Common Era the perception of Ethiopia as an "end of the earth" was firmly entrenched. Strabo's *Geography of Strabo*, called one of the most important geographical works ever produced by any Greek or Roman writer (and representing the first attempt to condense all geographical knowledge attainable) (Kish, 85; Bunbury, II: 209-293), preserved this perception. Strabo assumed, like geographers before him, that the southern shore of Libya was surrounded by "Ocean," with the southernmost limit of the world extending "3000 stadia below Meroë" (Strabo 1.2.27-28; 2.2.2.). Strabo identified the Ethiopia as the southernmost region of the world:

> I maintain . . . that in accordance with the opinion of the ancient Greeks--just as they embraced the inhabitants of the known countries of the north under the single designation "Scythians" . . . and just as later, when the inhabitants of the west also were discovered, they were called Celts . . . I maintain, I say, that just so, in accordance with the opinion of the ancient Greeks, *all the countries in the south which lie on Oceanus were called Ethiopia*." (Strabo 1.2.27, italics mine)

We would argue that the Ethiopian's geographical provenance was, like his ethnographical identity, of particular significance for Luke, and not parenthetical minutiae. It is extremely plausible that when the Lucan community read about a story of an "Ethiopian" returning home southward to a region located on the edge of "Ocean," they would have considered that the Gospel had reached the "end of the earth" in that instance--a partial fulfillment of the prophetic and programmatic statement in Acts 1:8c. Thus, the Ethiopian's return home

---

[24] Herodotus recognized a division of the world into three continents: Europe, Asia, and Libya (Africa). Egypt belonged to Asia, and Libya was surrounded by the sea on all sides except where it joined to Asia. "Arabia" was the most distant country to the southeast, Ethiopia the most distant to the southwest. Cf. Herodotus 3.107.

represents not only the extension of the Gospel beyond Israel to the Gentile world--it represents the symbolic (and partial) fulfillment of Acts 1:8c of mission "to the end of the earth." The Ethiopian's geographical provenance uniquely qualifies him to represent this fulfillment.

Interpretation for Liberation and the "Politics of Omission"

We have shown that while elements of the Ethiopian treasurer's "theological" significance in Acts 8:26-40 are readily acceded (e.g., the prophecy-fulfillment function), the significance of his geographical--and especially his ethnographical--provenance receive far less attention and explicit analysis. At least three factors are proposed as contributing to this proclivity in the history of the interpretation of the pericope.

First, there is an "internal" phenomenon operative within the ideological framework of the New Testament itself which tends to circumscribe any detailed and expansive attention to Ethiopians *per se*. Cain H. Felder's analysis of "secularization" in the New Testament is especially useful for our consideration here. In his provocative study "Racial Ambiguities in the Biblical Narratives," Felder defines "secularization" as the process by which the socio-political realities of the secular framework of the Christian authors in the New Testament led to a marginalization of the darker races. Specifically, the socio-political character of Rome as comprising a new and increasingly hegemonic center and symbol of the new center of God's redemptive activity (in contradistinction to Jerusalem) culminated in the perception of Rome as "the ultimate destination of the Christian kerygma . . . the new focus of the Christian missionary movement" (22). The confession of the Roman centurion in Mark's gospel, for example, is situated as a major narrative climax in the story.[25] Luke's numerous allusions to "centurions" as positive, pious figures is also well-known (Lk. 7:2ff; 23:47; Acts 10:1-11:18; 21:30-32; 22:25-28; 24:23ff; 27:42-44; 28:16). The significance of this increasing focus on Rome (certainly in the period post-70 C.E.) instead of Jerusalem is that "the darker races outside the Roman orbit are circumstantially marginalized by New Testament authors . . . socio-political realities of the secular framework tend to dilute the New Testament vision of racial inclusiveness and universalism" (22). There is, in short, a decided ideological and geographical shift from the southeastern region of the Mediterranean world to the northwest region.

---

[25] Mk. 15:39, 44, 45. Felder notes: "It is no coincidence that Mark, the earliest composer of the Passion Narrative, goes to such great lengths to show that the confession of the Roman centurion . . . brings his whole gospel to a climax" (22).

A second and more contemporary "external" phenomenon which contributes to a general lack of familiarity with "Ethiopians" and their provenance for twentieth century students of the Bible is the failure of many Bible atlases to include the region south of Palestine and Egypt in its illustrations. Of the useful atlases recommended by Joseph A. Fitzmyer in his excellent reference work, *An Introductory Bibliography for the Study of Scripture*, the majority do not include Meroë (or Nubai) in their maps of the world of the New Testament. An exception is the map "The Roman World at the Birth of Jesus" provided in George E. Wright and Floyd V. Filson's *The Westminster Historical Atlas to the Bible*.[26]

In its maps of the New Testament world the *Oxford Bible Atlas* depicts the northern region of Egypt as far south as Thebes and Hierakonpolis on its map entitled "The Near East," but one nowhere learns of the existence of Meroë in the maps concerned with the New Testament period--even the map optimistically entitled "The Background of the New Testament" omits this region. It is to the maps depicting the Old Testament world that one must turn to situate Meroë in the ancient world in this volume (May, 1984:67).

It may be objected that "Ethiopia" should not be included in maps of the Roman Empire, since technically, it is not located within the geographical confines of the Empire; however, one may also argue that maps which purport to include regions reflective of the expanding evangelistic outreach of the Church (such as a map entitled "The Background of the New Testament") should, in fact, depict those regions to which New Testament narrative texts allude.

Finally, we propose that presumptions of the Ethiopian's ethnographic identity as "marginally significant" or "inconsequential" for the Lucan theological perspective altogether may be traced to a larger and perennial problem in Western, post-Enlightenment culture wherein the signification and contributions of particular groups of persons have been historically marginalized or ignored. This ideological, psycho-social and cultural marginalization and "omission" continues to foster an "opaque" and, in this instance, culturally or ethnically proscribed prism through which the biblical reader and interpreter envisions and ascertains which data are "theologically significant" within a biblical text.

---

[26] Plate XIII. Cf. L.H. Grollenberg (32); Pauline Lemaire and P. Donato Baldi, Map XII. But Yohanan Aharoni and Michael Avi-Yonah do include an illustration demarcating the region near Gaza where Philip would have encountered the Ethiopian. See Map 241. We are not engaging in historical reconstruction here, arguing that the story comes to us as objective history; nonetheless, we note that Nubia's significance in the Lucan theological framework in Acts 8:26-40 is such that students of the Bible should be familiar with the geographical designations mentioned in the pericope.

One illustration of this tendency to "marginalize" or treat as "inconsequential" the significance of, for example, racial minorities in ancient and modern literature may be seen in the treatment of the "black" or "black African" in antiquity in general. In this regard Frank M. Snowden correctly calls into question the shocking dearth of documentary studies on Ethiopians in classical antiquity. Snowden observes that while Greeks and Romans were familiar with Ethiopians, modern scholarship has failed to relate archaeological and literary materials in a way which informs and enlarges our understanding of their status and involvements in Greco-Roman society:

> The Greeks and Romans knew a great deal about the physical features of the peoples whom they called Ethiopians. Their writers described the Ethiopian type in considerable detail. From the hands of their artists we have received an ever more copious evidence which shows in a vivid manner the racial characteristics of many Ethiopian inhabitants of the Greco-Roman world. *Hence it is surprising that modern scholarship has virtually ignored Greek and Roman anthropological knowledge of the Ethiopian.* (1, italics mine)

Racial minorities and women in particular have challenged epistemological, analytical and interpretive constructs in modern academic discourse which render them invisible. In recent years, for example, female scholars in every academic discipline have been engaged in the assiduous--but inspiring--task of recovering and reconstructing women's history. The general exclusion of women as both producers and subjects of knowledge (Spender: 1) and the consequential "muteness" of women, has perpetuated an "invisibility" of women and delegitimated women as subordinates and marginals. Schüssler Fiorenza reminds us that the urgency with which women are challenging the silence about women in historiography, literature, sociology, and the human sciences represents more than a "compensatory" undertaking--it represents--a "paradigm shift" from an androcentric world-view to an inclusive feminist comprehension of the world, human life, and history (1984:2). Jane Lewis concludes correctly that the writers of the "new women's history" have in recent decades been "fired with the dual purpose of restoring women to history and history to women" (55). Two titles which capture this passion and collaborative effort to reverse the ongoing consequences of the "politics of omission" in the lives of women are appropriately named: *Hidden from History* (Rowbotham) and *Becoming Visible: Women in European History* (Bridenthal and Koonz).

A priori assumptions of the "inconsequential" nature of the Ethiopian's ethnographic identity--whether conscious or unconscious, intentional or unintentional--are too often consonant with interpretive formulations which automatically assign a diminished valuation to the ethnographic significance of "blacks" or "black Africans" in general. In his impressive survey of the role of discursive factors in the codification of white supremacist ideals in the pre- and post-Enlightenment age, Cornel West argues that a combination of scientific investigation, Cartesian epistemology (wherein Descartes' emphasis on the primacy of the subject and the preeminence of "representation" became a controlling notion of modern discourse), and classical ideals "produced forms of rationality, scientificity, and objectivity which, though efficacious in the quest for truth and knowledge, prohibited the intelligibility and legitimacy of the idea of black equality in beauty, culture, and intellectual capacity. In fact, to think such an idea was to be deemed irrational, barbaric, or mad" (64). There is no dearth of literature on the subject of how these and other similarly negative ideological formulations have contributed to the invisibility, marginalization and omission of "black" persons in postmodern American literature and culture.[27]

In his important discussion of the role of "ideological suspicion" in the hermeneutical task in biblical interpretation and theology, Juan Luis Segundo observes that our way of experiencing reality leads us to "ideological suspicion" as we approach and interpret biblical texts. Four decisive factors are operative in this epistemic construct. First, one's way of experiencing reality prompts an "ideological suspicion;" secondly, an individual applies the "ideological suspicion" to the whole ideological superstructure (within the context of our discussion, theology receives particular focus); third, a new way of experiencing theological reality arises which leads to an "exegetical suspicion" that a prevailing interpretation of the Bible "*has not taken important pieces of data into account;*" and fourth, the interpretation of Scripture (the "fountainhead" of our faith) proceeds in new ways allowing the exegete to incorporate the new elements into his or her ideological superstructure" (9).

Elisabeth Schüssler Fiorenza's extended analysis of the centrality of a "hermeneutics of suspicion" in feminist biblical interpretation provides a useful heuristic model for ascertaining ways in which a "hermeneutics of suspicion" can be utilized in assessing biblical interpretations wherein ethnographic data (which may illumine dimensions of a biblical writer's theological perspective in historical biblical criticism) has, in fact, been minimized or ignored. A critical point

---

[27] The literature of this subject is too massive to reproduce here, but see, for example, Wilmore and Cone; C.E. Lincoln; and for a helpful overview of the impact of racial formulations on American culture see: Winthrop Jordan.

of departure in the methodology of a "feminist hermeneutics of suspicion" is the admission that no interpretation or scholarship is "objective," "intellectually neutral," or "value free," for the exegete always brings his or her own presuppositions, assumptions, and subjectivity to the interpretive process (1984:98, 118, 132, 137).[28] Schüssler Fiorenza notes: "A feminist hermeneutics of suspicion questions underlying presuppositions, androcentric models, and inarticulated interests of contemporary biblical interpretation" (1984:16). It tests ways, for example, in which contemporary biblical interpretation promotes "linguistic sexism" which "creates the linguistic invisibility and marginality of women, characterizes them in stereotypical roles and images, and trivializes their contributions" (1984:17). Taking as its starting point the assumption that biblical texts are androcentric and serve patriarchal functions, feminist critical interpretation searches for the "lost traditions and visions of liberation" in androcentric biblical texts and interpretations in the same way that the woman in the parable sweeps the whole house in search of her lost coin:

> In order to unearth a "feminist coin" from the biblical tradition it critically analyzes contemporary scholarly and popular interpretations, the tendencies of the biblical writers and traditioning processes themselves, and the theoretical models underlying contemporary biblical historical and theological interpretations (1984:16).

The "search" which a feminist hermeneutic of suspicion engenders tests both the original biblical text and contemporary interpretations and translations of the text, thereby clarifying and exposing "hidden" presuppositions, assumptions and convictions operative in historical, critical methodology. Further, it incorporates both a cultural and theological critique (1983:21).

Segundo and Schüssler Fiorenza's analyses of the role of a "hermeneutic of suspicion" in biblical interpretation are instructive in assessing the issues at stake in the minimalization or omission of the significance of the Ethiopian's ethnographic and geographic provenance in Acts 8:26-40.

---

[28] That "presuppositionless" exegesis is impossible is well-established in scholarly literature on hermeneutics. In Richard Palmer's word: "All explanatory interpretation is made within a horizon of already granted meanings and intentions. In hermeneutics, this area of assumed understanding is called pre-understanding" (24). The nature of the hermeneutical task is such that both text and interpreter are conditioned by their respective place in history. For other helpful discussions of the function of presuppositions in interpretation cf. Thiselton and Lundin, Thiselton, Walhout, *inter alia*.

Just as Gealy and Dahl's conclusions should trigger "hermeneutical suspicions" regarding the historical treatment of the Ethiopian's ethnographic and geographic provenance in biblical research in Acts 8:26-40, so should they prompt a more critical stance toward interpretations of other pericopae which allude to "historically marginalized persons"--including women and "blacks" (African)-- in the Hebrew Bible and the New Testament. Notions of what constitutes "significant" data continue to be applied selectively to historical sources and data in accordance with the theoretical models or perspectives which order an interpreter's information (Schüssler Fiorenza, 1984:99). When the ethnographic and geographic significance of the Ethiopian eunuch is relegated to the "back heap" of trivial minutiae and literary ornamentation, it is possible to miss the richness and breadth of theological data in biblical interpretation.

It is true that the Ethiopian eunuch was not a twentieth century Afro-American male, but C. Eric Lincoln has correctly noted that, in Afro-American communities at least, the story of a black African convert to Christianity continues to comprise a culturally affirming and empowering tradition. Afro-Americans, whose experience of, in his words, a "white American Christianity" which has legitimized psycho-social and cultural marginalization in both church and society, are eager and "determined" to reclaim an ancient biblical heritage which "avoids the embarrassments of brotherly denigration in America," and helps Afro-Americans to "reestablish their connection with the faith at its inception" (Lincoln, 24). Lincoln argues that the explicit allusion to the Gospel promise extending to black Africa in Acts 8:26-40 should not be overlooked:

> But as if to underscore the divine intention that black Africa (which first touched the destiny of Israel when Abraham came out of Ur and settled in Egypt, and continued through all the centuries thereafter) should be a direct and unequivocal heir to that promise, after Pentecost, the divine imperative came to the evangelist Philip, directing him toward a rendezvous which made inevitable the inclusion of black Africans among the charter members of the faith . . . an African nobleman . . . received the good news from his lips, and accepted baptism at his hand (Acts 8:26-39), all of which symbolizes from the beginning the African involvement in the new faith that was to spread throughout the world (24).

If the ongoing process of interpreting biblical traditions is to be in any sense "interpretation for liberation"--that is, interpretation which effects full humanity, empowerment, and justice in church and society under God--interpreters must continue to critically discern ways in which a "politics of omission" may be operative in perpetuating the marginalization and "invisibility" of traditionally marginalized persons, groups, and ideologies in biblical narratives. It is only as we undertake such critical analyses that a potentially liberatory vision of biblical traditions can emerge and function as an empowering force in *all* contemporary communities of faith.

WORKS CONSULTED

Adams, William Y.
    1964   "Post-Pharonic Nubia in the Light of Archaeology, I." *JEA* 50:102-20.
    1965   "Post-Pharonic Nubia in the Light of Archaeology, II." *JEA* 51:160-78.
    1977   *Nubia: Corridor to Africa.* Princeton: Princeton University Press.

Aharoni, Yohanan and Michael Avi-Yonah.
    1968   *The Macmillan Bible Atlas.* New York: Macmillan.

Anderson, A.A.
    1983   *The Book of the Psalms.* NCB. Vol. I. Grand Rapids: Eerdmans.

Arndt, William F. and F. Wilbur Gingrich.
    1973   *A Greek-English Lexicon of the New Testament and Other Early Christian Literature.* Chicago: University of Chicago Press.

Aus, Roger D.
    1979   "Paul's Travel Plans to Spain and the 'Full Number of the Gentiles' of Rom. XI 25." *NT* 11, fasc. 3:232-62.

Ball, John.
    1942   *Egypt in the Classical Geographers.* Cairo: Government Press, Bulâq.

Beardsley, G.H.
    1929   *The Negro in Greek and Roman Civilization.* Baltimore, Johns Hopkins.

Bovon, François.
    1978   *Luc le théologien: Vingt-cinq ans de recherches (1950-1975).* Paris: Delchaux and Niestlé Editeurs.

Bridenthal, Renate and Claudia Koonz, eds.
1977   *Becoming Visible: Women in European History.* Boston: Houghton Mifflin.

Brinkman, J.A.
1963   "The Literary Background of the 'Catalogue of Nations,' Acts 2, 9-11."*CBQ* 25:418-27.

Brodie, Thomas L.
1986   "Towards Unraveling the Rhetorical Imitation of Sources in Acts: 2 Kings 5 as One Component of Acts 8, 9-40." *Bib* 67:41-67.

Bruce, F.F.
1976   *The Book of the Acts.* NICNT. Grand Rapids: Eerdmans.
1984   *The Acts of the Apostles: The Greek Text with Introduction and Commentary.* Grand Rapids: Eerdmans.

Bunbury, E.H.
1959   *A History of Ancient Geography Among the Greeks and Romans From Earliest Ages Till the Fall of the Roman Empire.* 2 vols. New York: Dover Publications. First edition: New York: Century: 1932.

Cadbury, H.J.
1955   *The Book of Acts in History.* New York: Harper and Brothers.
1979   "The Hellenists." Pp. 59-74 in *Beg. V.* Ed. F.J. Foakes-Jackson and Kirsopp Lake. First edition. London: Macmillan, 1920-1933.

Comstock, Mary B. and Cornelius C. Vermule.
1976   *Sculpture in Stone: The Greek, Roman and Etruscan Collections of the Museum of Fine Arts, Boston.* Boston: Museum of Fine Arts.

Courtès, Jean Marie.
1979   "The Theme of 'Ethiopia' and 'Ethiopians' in Patristic Literature." Pp. 9-32 in *The Image of the Black in Western Art: From the Early Christian Church to the Age of Discovery.* Vol. 2, Pt. 1. Ed. Ladislas Bugner. New York: William Morrow.

Dahl, Nils A.
1974   "Nations in the New Testament." Pp. 54-68 in *New Testament Christianity for Africa and the World: Essays in Honor of Harry Sawyer.* Ed. Mark E. Glaswell and Edward Fashole-Luke. London: SPCK.
1980   "The Story of Abraham in Luke-Acts." Pp. 139-158 in *Studies in Luke-Acts.* Ed. Leander Keck and J. Louis Martyn. Philadelphia: Fortress.

Dahood, Mitchell.
1983   *Psalms II: 51-100: Introduction Translation, and Notes.* AB. New York: Doubleday.

Desanges, Jehan.
1976   "The Iconography of the Black in Ancient North Africa." Pp. 246-268 in *The Image of the Black in Western Art. From the Pharoan to the Fall of the Roman Empire.* Vol. 1. Ed. Ladislas Bugner. New York: William Morrow.

Dibelius, Martin.
1956   *Studies in the Acts of the Apostles.* New York: Charles Scribner's Sons.

Dodd, C.H.
1952   *According to the Scriptures: The Substructure of New Testament Theology.* London: Nisbet.

Dupont, Jacques.
1953a   *Les Actes Des Apôtres.* Paris: Les Editions Du Cerf.
1953b   "L'utilization apologetique de l'ancien Testament dans les discours des Actes." *ETL* 29:289-327.

Felder, Cain.
1982   "Racial Ambiguities in the Biblical Narratives." Pp. 17-24 in *The Church and Racism.* Concilium 151. Ed. Gregory Baum and John Coleman. New York: Seabury.

Finn, David and Caroline Houser.
1983   *Greek Monumental Bronze Sculpture.* New York: Vendome.

Fitzmyer, Joseph A.
1981a   *An Introductory Bibliography for the Study of Scripture.* Subsidia Biblica 3. Revised edition. Rome: Biblical Institute Press.
1981b   *The Gospel According to Luke: A New Translation with Introduction and Commentary.* AB. 2 vols. New York: Doubleday.

Foakes-Jackson, F.J.
1931   *The Acts of the Apostles.* New York: Harper and Brothers.

Gealy, F.D.
1962   "Ethiopian Eunuch." Pp. 177-178 in *IDB*, vol. 1. 4 vols. Ed. George A. Buttrick. Nashville: Abingdon.

Godley, A.D. trans.
1928   *Herodotus.* 4 vols. LCL. New York: G.P. Putnam's Sons.

Grassi, Joseph A.
1964 "Emmaus Revisited (Luke 24, 13-35 and Acts 8, 26-40)." *CBQ* 26: 463-467.

Green, Michael.
1970 *Evangelism in the Early Church*. Grand Rapids: Eerdmans.

Grollenberg, L.H.
1960 *Atlas to the Bible. A Commentary*. Trans. and ed. Joyce M.H. Reid and H.H. Rowley. New York: Thomas Nelson.

Haenchen, Ernest.
1971 *The Acts of the Apostles: A Commentary*. Philadelphia: Westminster.

Hengel, Martin.
1979 *Acts and the History of Earliest Christianity*. Philadelphia: Fortress.

Hoad, T.F., ed.
1986 *The Concise Oxford Dictionary of English Etymology*. Oxford: At the Clarendon Press.

Jervell, Jacob.
1972 "The Divided People of God: The Restoration of Israel and the Salvation of the Gentiles." Pp. 41-74 in *Luke and the People of God: A New Look at Luke-Acts*. Minneapolis: Augsburg.

Jones, Horace Leonard, trans.
1932 *The Geography of Strabo*. LCL. 8 vols. New York: G.P. Putnam's Sons.

Jordan, Winthrop.
1968 *White Over Black: American Attitudes Toward the Negro, 1550-1812*. New York: W.W. Norton.

Karris, Robert J.
1978 *Invitation to Acts: A Commentary on the Acts of the Apostles with Complete Text from the Jerusalem Bible*. New York: Image Books.
1979 *What Are They Saying About Luke-Acts?* New York: Paulist.

Kish, George, ed.
1978 *A Sourcebook in Ancient Geography*. Cambridge: Harvard University Press.

Kurz, William B.
    1976   "The Function of Christological Proof From Prophecy for Luke and Justin." Ph.D. Dissertation, Yale University.
    1982   *The Acts of the Apostles.* Collegeville, MN: Liturgical Press.

Lawrence, William Frank.
    1984   "The History of the Interpretation of Acts 8:26-40 by the Church Fathers Prior to the Fall of Rome." Ph.D. Dissertation, Union Theological Seminary.

Lemaire, Pauline et P. Donato Baldi.
    1960   *Atlas Biblique. Histoire and géographie de la Bible.* Louvain: Editions Du Mont César.

Lewis, Jane.
    1981   "Women, Lost and Found: The Impact of Feminism on History." Pp. 55-72 in *Men's Studies Modified: The Impact of Feminism in the Academic Disciplines.* The Athene Series. Ed. Dale Spender. New York: Pergamon.

Liddell, H.G., and R. Scott.
    1961   *A Greek-English Lexicon: A New Edition Revised and Augmented Throughout.* Ed. Henry H.S. Jones with the assistance of Robert McKenzie. Oxford: At the Clarendon Press.

Lincoln, C.E.
    1984   *Race, Religion, and the Continuing American Dilemma.* New York: Hill and Wang.

Lindars, Barnabas.
    1961   *New Testament Apologetic: The Doctrinal Significance of the Old Testament Quotations.* Philadelphia: Westminster.

Lindijer, C.H.
    1978   "Two Creative Encounters in the Work of Luke: Luke xxiv 13-35 and Acts viii 26-40." *Miscellanea Neotestamentica* 94:77-85.

Lohse, E.
    1954   "Lukas als Theologe der Heilsgeschichte." *EvT* 14:256-275.

Loisy, Alfred.
    1920   *Les Actes Des Apôtres.* Paris. Émile Nourry.

Lundin, Roger, Anthony Thiselton and Clarence Walhout.
    1985   *The Responsibility of Hermeneutics.* Grand Rapids: Eerdmans.

Marshall, I.H.
    1978   *Commentary on Luke: A Commentary on the Greek Text*. NIGC. Grand Rapids: Eerdmans.
    1983   *The Acts of the Apostles*. TynNTC. Grand Rapids: Eerdmans.

Martin, Clarice J.
    1985   "The Function of Acts 8:26-40 Within the Narrative Structure of the Book of Acts: The Significance of the Eunuch's Provenance for Acts 1:8c." Ph.D. Dissertation. Duke University.

May, H.G. and B.M. Metzger.
    1977   *The New Oxford Annotated Bible with the Apocrypha*. Revised Standard Version: Containing the Second Edition of the New Testament and an Expanded Edition of the Apocrypha. New York/London: Oxford University.

May, Herbert G., ed.
    1984   *Oxford Bible Atlas*. 3rd ed. New York/London: Oxford University.

Metzger, Bruce M.
    1970   "Ancient Astrological Geography in Acts 2:9-11." Pp. 123-133 in *Apostolic History and the Gospel*. Ed. W. Ward Gasque and Ralph P. Martin. Grand Rapids: Eerdmans.

Mínguez, Dionisio.
    1976   "Hechos 8:25-40. Anàlisis estructural del relato." *Bib* 57, 2:168-191.

Munck, Johannes.
    1981   *The Acts of the Apostles*. AB. New York: Doubleday.

Murphy, Roland E.
    1968   "Psalms." Pp. 569-602 in *JBC*. Englewood Cliffs, NJ: Prentice-Hall.

Murray, A.T. trans.
    1960a   *The Odyssey*. 2 vols. LCL. Cambridge: Harvard University Press.
    1960b   *The Iliad*. 2 vols. LCL. Cambridge: Harvard University Press.

Navone, John.
    1978   *Themes of St. Luke*. Rome: Gregorian University Press.

O'Toole, Robert F.
    1983   "Philip and the Ethiopian Eunuch (Acts VIII 25-40)." *JSNT* 17:25-34.

1984	*The Unity of Luke's Theology: An Analysis of Luke-Acts.* Good News Studies 9. Wilmington, DE: Michael Glazier.

Palmer, Richard.
1969	*Hermeneutics. Interpretation Theory in Schleiermacher, Dilthey, Heidegger, and Gadamer.* Studies in Phenomenology and Existential Philosophy. Evanston: Northwestern University Press.

Partridge, Eric.
1966	*Origins: A Short Etymological Dictionary of Modern English.* London: Routledge and Kegan Paul.

Polhill, John B.
1974	"The Hellenistic Breakthrough: Acts 6-12." RE 71: 475-486.

Rackham, R.B.
1939	*The Acts of the Apostles: An Exposition.* London: Methuen.

Reicke, Bo.
1959	"Glaube und Leben der Urgemeinde. Bemerkungen zu Apg. 1-7." Pp. 9-37 in *Abhandlungen zur Theologie des Alten und Neuen Testaments* 32. Zürich: Zwingli-Verlag.

Rowbotham, Sheila.
1973	*Hidden From History.* London: Pluto.

Säve-Söderbergh, Torgny.
1987	*Temples and Tombs of Ancient Nubia.* New York: Thames and Hudson.

Schaff, Philip, *ed.*
1956	*Saint Augustine: Expositions on the Book of Psalms. A Select Library of the Nicene and Post-Nicene Fathers of the Christian Church.* Vol. 8. Grand Rapids: Eerdmans.

Schubert, Paul.
1957	"The Structure and Significance of Luke 24." Pp. 165-186 in *Neutestamentliche Studien fur Rudolf Bultmann.* Ed. W. Eltester. Berlin: Töpelmann.

Schüssler Fiorenza, Elisabeth.
1983	*In Memory of Her: A Feminist Reconstruction of Christian Origins.* New York: Crossroad.
1984	*Bread Not Stone: The Challenge of Feminist Biblical Interpretation.* Boston: Beacon.

Segundo, Juan Luis.
    1976   *The Liberation of Theology.* Trans. John Drury. New York: Orbis.

Selwyn, E.C.
    1911-A   "The Carefulness of Luke: III. Philip and the Eunuch." *Expos* I: 273-284.

Shinnie, Margaret.
    1965   *Ancient African Kingdoms.* London: Edward Arnold.

Snowden, Frank M., Jr.
    1976a   "Ethiopians in the Greco-Roman World." Pp. 11-36 in *The African Diaspora: Interpretive Essays.* Ed. Martin L. Kilson and Robert I. Rottberg. Cambridge: Harvard University Press.
    1976b   "Iconographical Evidence on the Black Populations in Greco-Roman Antiquity." Pp. 133-245 in *The Image of the Black in Western Art. From the Pharoah to the Fall of the Roman Empire.* Vol. I. Ed. Ladislas Bugner. New York: William Morrow.
    1979   *Blacks in Antiquity: Ethiopians in the Greco-Roman Experience.* Cambridge: Harvard University Press.

Spender, Dale, ed.
    1981   *Men's Studies Modified: The Impact of Feminism in the Academic Disciplines.* The Athene Series. New York: Pergamon.

Squillaci, D.
    1960   "La conversion dell' Ethiope (Atti 8, 26-40)." *Palestra del Clero* 39:1197-1201.

Talbert, Charles H.
    1984   "Promise and Fulfillment in Lucan Theology." Pp. 91-103, in *Luke-Acts: New Perspectives from the Society of Biblical Literature Seminar.* Ed. Charles H. Talbert. New York: Crossroad.

Thiselton, Anthony C.
    1980   *The Two Horizons: New Testament Hermeneutics and Philosophical Description.* Grand Rapids: Eerdmans.

Thompson, Robert, trans.
    1977   *Athanasius Syriaca: Expositio in Psalmos.* Corpus Scriptorum Christianorum Orientalium. Vol. 387. Louvain: Secretariat du Corpussco.

Thornton, T.C.G.
1977 "To the end of the earth: Acts 1:8." *ET* 89:374-75.

Tiede, D.L. *Prophecy and History in Luke-Acts.* Philadelphia: Fortress.
1980

Trocmé, Etienne.
1957 *"Le Livre Des Actes" Et L'Histoire.* Paris: Presses Universitaires De France.

Ullendorf, Edward.
1968 *Ethiopia and the Bible.* London: Oxford University Press.

Van Unnik, W.C.
1973 "Der Ausdruck "ΕΩΣ 'ΕΣΧΑΤΟΥ ΤΗΣ ΓΗΣ' (Apostelgeschicte 1 8) Und Sein Alttestamentlicher Hintergrund." Pp. 386-401 in *Sparsa Collecta. The Collected Essays of W.C. Van Unnik.* Pt. I. Evangelia-Paulina-Acta. *NovTSup* 29. Leiden: E.J. Brill.

Weinstock, Stefan.
1948 "The Geographical Catalogue in Acts II, 9-11." *JRS* 38:44-46.

West, Cornel.
1982 *Prophesy Deliverance! An Afro-American Revolutionary Christianity.* Philadelphia: Westminster.

Westermann, Claus.
1975 *Isaiah 40-66.* NCB. London: Oliphants.

Williams, C.S.C.
1964 *A Commentary on the Acts of the Apostles.* London: Adam and Charles Black.

Wilmore, Gayraud S. and James Cone.
1979 *Black Theology: A Documentary History, 1966-1979.* New York: Orbis.

Wilson, S.G.
1973 *The Gentiles and the Gentile Mission in Luke-Acts.* Studiorum Novi Testamenti Societas, Monograph Series 23. New York/London: Cambridge University Press.

Wright, George E. and Floyd Vivian Filson, eds.
1956 *The Westminster Historical Atlas to the Bible.* Revised Edition. Philadelpha: Westminster.

Young, Edward J.
    1949   "Of Whom Speaketh the Prophet This?" *WTJ* 11:133-55.

Zahn, Theodor.
    1922   *Die Apostelgeschichte des Lucas: Erste Hälfte kap 1-12.* Leipzig: A. Deichertsche Vorlagsbuch-handlung.

Ziegler, Joseph, ed.
    1939   *Isaias.* Septuaginta Vetus Testamentum Graecum Auctoritate Societastis Litterarum Gottingensis editum. Vol. 14. Göttingen: Vandenhoeck and Ruprecht.

CAN AN ENSLAVED GOD LIBERATE?
HERMENEUTICAL REFLECTIONS ON
PHILIPPIANS 2:6-11

Sheila Briggs
University of Southern California

The Voice of the Oppressed Under the Text

Any serious biblical hermeneutics of liberation must reflect on the fact that the reading of biblical texts as warrants for political and socio-economic oppression is not misinterpretation of a few pericopes isolated form their context. One is also not helped by conceding that the intention of the original authors of *some* texts was—as far as this is recoverable—the support of hierarchical social structures of the time, but then denying that it is typical of the biblical witness. The problem of the biblical text for a hermeneutics of liberation does not result from earlier generations of interpreters having chosen as *loci communes* for a biblical understanding of society a group of texts which does not represent the consensus of biblical writings. Such claims ignore the embeddedness of the biblical texts in both material reality and in human consciousness. The reproduction of oppressive social structures in a religious text shapes an imaginative matrix which underlies all utterances of that text. The hermeneutical problem exists prior to the text in the origins of the text. If members of a dominant social group have been in control of the process of canonization of biblical texts, then it is hardly surprising that their beliefs, values and interests are enshrined in the text to which they have assigned religious authority. Elisabeth Schüssler Fiorenza has argued that the canon of the New Testament preserves writings, formulated and selected from an androcentric perspective. One can talk of more or less androcentric texts but only with the recognition that androcentrism pervades the whole of the New Testament. Behind the text of the New Testament we can catch glimpses of early Christian egalitarian traditions which were lost through the process of transmission and canonization in an increasingly patriarchal church.

There are three categories of texts which pose different sets of problems for a biblical hermeneutics of liberation. There are the texts which point behind the text in the sense that the process of redaction and canonization has not completely erased the voice of the oppressed. The task is therefore to reconstruct the historical circumstances and expressions of the oppressed. Since this enterprise will always be limited by the repression and accidental loss of the documentary and other evidence of the lives and mental universes of the oppressed, we are faced with the question of whether we should invent a past which we cannot recover. Charges of anachronism are out of place here as long as one maintains a strict demarcation between the two methods employed. Indeed, the truth-status of an invented past is not necessarily more restricted in terms of empirical proof than that of a conventional historical hypothesis. Both present us with *possible* pasts and both need to be submitted to the same type of hermeneutical controls, which cannot be derived from empirical tests of fact. The reason for this is that all historical judgments rest upon *analogy*. We make inferences from present experience as to what was possible for human beings in the past to have experienced. Such inferences are loaded with presuppositions of a wide variety—religious, metaphysical, anthropological, etc. Consequently the initial step in the hermeneutical process, that of clarification of the presuppositions which form our pre-understanding of a text or any object of interpretation, must precede every historical reconstruction, whether conventional or imaginative.

The second category of texts are those which give voice to the beliefs, values and interests of the dominant social group. The approach of a biblical hermeneutics of liberation to this class of texts is that of ideology-critique. The task of historical reconstruction is easier here because of the relative abundance of evidence which has been transmitted to us, due in part to the desire of later élites to trace their genealogy back to the earlier group and hence having had a motive to preserve its records. Yet, the abundance of this evidence over against that which perpetuates the memory of the oppressed creates a hermeneutical problem for a liberation perspective. It can be said, for instance, of antiquity and of most historical periods that men's views about women rather than women's lives have been more accessible to the historian. Quite often the reconstruction of the conditions, roles and attitudes of the oppressed can only take place by trying to remove the suppression of the oppressed's reality in the discourse of their oppressors. Unlike in the case of the first category of texts this suppression is original to all historical levels of the text. Moreover, what we have here consists of the *perceptions* of the oppressors. We must allow not only for deliberate distortion of social reality but also for the possibility that it was misconceived. We cannot assume that a social élite always *knows* its interests, even less that it acts upon them. Its behavior is always subject to non-rational constraints in the sense that these are not derived from an empirical assessment of utility. One class of non-rational constraints is religious beliefs. Furthermore, the creators of the New Testament canon were an *alienated* social élite. In the first three centuries of Christianity any member of the dominant social groups who joined a scorned and proscribed sect must have suffered some degree of social alienation. Many of the Church Fathers refused participation in the institutions (the slave-holding patriarchal household, imperial government, etc.) which they upheld. The perceptions of an alienated segment of the social élites, whose judgments were permeated by the non-rational considerations of religious belief, can hardly be accounted accurate expressions of the instrumental rationality of the oppressor classes of the Greco-Roman world, and likewise they are unlikely to give an unerring description of the oppressed groups that opposed these.

The third category of texts occasions most difficulty to a biblical hermeneutics of liberation. These are texts of which it is unclear whether their *effect* on the original communities and individuals who heard, wrote and read them was conserving of the oppressive social order or produced criticism of and dissatisfaction with it, and even some measure of action towards transformation. This ambiguity in the texts cannot be resolved by postulating that they are of a mixed variety, expressing the beliefs, values and interests of both the oppressed and the oppressor. The intentions and even more so the unconscious motivations of the communities and individuals who produced the biblical texts are notoriously difficult to fathom, and this is especially so as regards this class of writings. Does the ambiguity that the text has in its effect upon social reality have its sources in the consciousness of those who produced it and (particularly in the case of liturgical texts) performed it? If the oppressed belonged to the community of producers and performers fo the biblical text, then the issue of "false consciousness" is raised. Yet, false consciousness seems to be more explanatory of historical fact than descriptive of consciousness. For example, since no social revolution succeeded in the Greco-Roman world it is deduced that the false consciousness of the oppressed was a tragic component in its failure. Another way to view the ambiguity of this class of texts would be to see in its multivalency a range of different performances, hearings, readings. That the performance of the text by the oppressor prevailed in its social world may be the result of the distribution of power rather than the false consciousness of the oppressed.

The Use of Analogy in Historical Reconstruction

The assertion that the multivalency of a biblical text allows different performances, hearings, readings does not lead to the conclusion that all are of equal value. From a liberation perspective a hermeneutical privilege of the oppressed is claimed. This claim can best be examined by further investigation of the role of analogy in historical reconstruction and its hermeneutical implications. The first characteristic of an analogy is that it attempts at statement about something unknown through comparison with that which is known. The use of analogy in historiography acknowledges the unknown quality of the past whilst avoiding a doctrine of its unknowability. The use of analogy very easily lends itself to the proposition that to the extent that the past is knowable it is not alien to the present. But a biblical hermeneutics of liberation has a stake in defending the alien character of the past in the sense that the past cannot be reduced to the epistemological structures of a present day society, where knowledge so often functions as a form of domination. The modern concept of history was the ideological product of an emergent bourgeois liberal society. It embodies the technical virtuoisty of this society including the competence to act as an instrument of control of its environment. It achieves control of the historical environment of the present by rendering the past transparent to the highest degree possible. Underlying such a project are assumptions about human nature, which are then universalized synchronically to other contemporary cultures and diachronically to other historical periods. Just as the Western development expert claims to know what the needs and desires of a Latin American peasant *qua* human being are, so the modern historian professes to hold a similar knowledge about what a slave in antiquity could have needed or desired as a human being.

Liberation theologies have, on the whole, uncritically adopted the modern concept of history. This is especially true of Latin American liberation theology, where salvation history (the theological counterpart of modern historical theory) has been fused with some aspects of Marxist historical materialism. Indeed, what has ensued is a struggle for control of the past between protagonists of liberation theologies and their opponents without the former asking whether such control reduplicates the oppressive structures of our own technocratic capitalism in historical discourse. The repercussion of this for a biblical hermeneutics of liberation is that the suppression of the voice of the oppressed in the text is repeated in interpretation. Within the contemporary world the *integrity* of the oppressed is emphasized from a liberation perspective. One maintains that the lives of the oppressed are not thoroughly amenable to manipulation through the knowledge of experts. The latter knowledge strives to approximate as far as possible a total understanding of the human person, particularly of those considered to be deviant, i.e., not sufficiently fulfilling the social roles assigned to them.

We need a corresponding notion of the integrity of persons in the past which explains our inability to understand the past not in terms of lack of evidence, nor on the basis that we lack the technical means to recover subjective mental processes of historical persons, but through appeal to the character of the hermeneutical process. Understanding cannot be reduced to a set of technical procedures which prepares the data of human lives to be objects of various enquiries. Instead, understanding has an intuitive component which can acknowledge, but not describe, dimensions of reality that cannot be empirically known. Therefore, we must reformulate the use of analogy in historiography to take into account the hermeneutic intuition and its respect for the integrity of the past. The analogy becomes the comparison between the *unknown* of the present and the unknown of the past, between that which eludes the deployment of knowledge as a means of social control in the present and that which in the past resisted the hegemony of the symbolic universe, prescribed by the social élites.

Although analogy must be used with caution in historical reconstruction it is indispensable, since even our recognition of a core of unknowable past experience depends upon it. Indeed, analogy in the strictest sense underlies hermeneutics, above all a hermeneutics of liberation. The *tertium comparationis* of the historiographical analogy is relationships: the social relationships of past societies and the social relationships of present society. In this it differs from an allegory. There is no direct comparison between persons and events in the past and those in the present. Certainly, a biblical hermeneutics of liberation, where it is practiced in the pastoral setting of a community of the oppressed such as the base communities of Latin America, tries to integrate oppressed Christians into the narrative universe of biblical texts, but his is not allied with an allegorical understanding of history. The Latin American and other liberation theologians do not look upon the bible as a series of codes which the oppressed on account of their hermeneutical privilege can "crack." The allegory, although full of concrete detail, undermines the concreteness of the persons and events described by assigning them meaning and value as the typical and not as the particular. A biblical hermeneutics of liberation, on the other hand, is concerned with their concreteness because social relationships cannot exist between abstract qualities. The terms oppressed and oppressor designate the concrete reality of a social relationship. There may be few or no direct similarities between groups of the oppressed, especially across time, but one can design models of oppression which can be analytically useful in cross-cultural or transhistorical comparisons. The oppressed are involved in a social relationship of dependence in which their status, power and rights are diminished or negated. Conversely, the liberation can be specified as a strategy to transform a social relationship so that it is not characterized by dependence or a disequilibrium of status, power and rights. A biblical hermeneutics of liberation makes an analogy between the social relationships or oppression/liberation in the past and those in the present. It cannot, therefore, claim a *direct* hermeneutical privilege of the oppressed since the configuration of concrete experiences of oppression and liberation remain unique and hence hermeneutically removed from all interpreters. Nonetheless, there is an indirect hermeneutical privilege of the oppressed, based on the knowability of the past being the analogical reconstruction of its social relationships. Such a claim rests itself, of course, on the notion, ultimately derived from Marx, that the oppressed—and not the oppressor—have an interest in recognizing the true nature of the social relationship, in which they are, so they can alter it. Since the contemporary oppressed know their own relationship of oppression and may seek their own liberation, they are more likely to make the analogy between their own experience and similar social relationships reproduced in the biblical texts.

A biblical hermeneutics of liberation employs simultaneously the historiographical analogy in its two distinct forms: the analogy between the elements of contemporary experience uncontrolled through social knowledge and the irrecoverable aspects of past experience, and the analogy between past and present social relationships. This method enables a fruitful approach to that class of biblical texts where the social effect is ambiguous.

Philippians 2:6-11: Christology and the Process of Enslavement

An important group in this category are some of the texts which draw their *theological* imagery from the social relationships of the patriarchal household (husband-wife, parent-child, master-slave). For example, Paul in his central reflection on sin, law and righteousness in Romans alternates between metaphors drawn from the master-slave relationship (Rom 6:20-22, 7:14) and those drawn from the social dyad of husband-wife (Rom 7:2-5). Paul's use of imagery taken from the patriarchal household is not without precedent. The pre-pauline hymn of Phil 2:6-11 makes its christological statement through the metaphor of slavery. The Philippians hymn appears to have its origin in a liturgical setting. Although we do not know who its original performers were, they probably shared the social diversity of early Christian communities and included both slaves and slave-holders. Did the slaves and the slave-holders endow this hymn with the same meaning and what effect did it have on their social relationship? Phil 2:6-11 thus provides an instructive trial of the hermeneutical method I have outlined.

The Philippians hymn recounts the self-abasement of Jesus Christ through becoming human and his death on the Cross and his subsequent exaltation by God to lord of the cosmos. The hymn produces its effect by drawing sharp contrasts between the three stages of Christ's original equality with God, his humiliation and death in human form and his final glorification as ruler of the cosmos. In v 6a one learns that Christ exists in the "form of God" (en morphę theou hyparchōn), yet he empties himself of his divinity and takes on the "form of a slave" (morphēn doulou labōv, v7b). The slave-existence of Christ's humanity stands in stark contrast to the acclamation of Christ's lordship at the end of the hymn (v11). "Jesus Christ is Lord" draws the strength of its metaphor not only from the relationship between hellenistic monarch and subject but also from that of the slaveowner as kurios of the slave. Christ is the doulos who has been made kurios, or has regained in enhanced form his original status as master.

Phil 2:7b is not *about* slavery as a social institution. It does not provide a critique of or an apology for slavery, nor does it attribute cosmic or soteriological significance to that institution through its description of Christ taking on the form of a slave. Yet, when one has established that Philippians does not contain a reference to the social institution of slavery, one is confronted with the fact that the material reality of that social relationship has been transformed into metaphor, that the cultural, including the religious, imagination of the Greco-Roman world is bounded by the mentality of a slave society. The humiliation of Christ in the "form of a slave" comprises two elements. Firstly, there is an obvious comparison between the lowly status of Christ's earthly existence and his original equality with God. However, the poignancy of the portrayal of Christ as slave derives not only from a loss of status but also from the degradation of being a slave. This sense of degradation is heightened by the assertion that it is a divine being who has become a slave, that the two opposites in the realm of being and worth have met in one person and one fate. Furthermore, the insistence on Christ's original equality with God points out that Christ's existence did not begin as that of a slave. In the ancient world it was forbidden by law to enslave free persons except as a penalty for crime. In addition, there were categories of persons considered too worthy to enslave. For example, the Greeks held it abhorrent to enslave fellow Greeks. The Philippians hymn conveys the extremity of the self-abasement of Christ by placing it in the metaphor of the enslavement of God. Christ as divine was absolutely too worthy to be enslaved.

To understand the theological reduplication of the social reality of slavery in Phil 2:6-11 two sets of categories, developed in the work of the sociologist Orlando Patterson, prove helpful. Enslavement, according to Patterson, entails *natal alienation* and *social death*. In societies, where slavery was practiced, one mode of conceptualizing it was to see it as a substitution for executing prisoners of war. Irrespective of whether all or most slaves in such a society were in fact prisoners of war, they were viewed as socially dead. Patterson outlines a general model of the slave's social death:

> The slave is violently uprooted from his milieu. He is desocialized and depersonalized. This process of social negation constitutes the first, essentially external, phase of enslavement. The next phase involves the introduction of the slave into the community of his master, but it involves the paradox of introducing him as a nonbeing (38).

Patterson notes that this conception of the slave as the outsider socially dead within society predominated in the Greco-Roman world. Against this background one can see that the contrast between Christ existing in the "form of God" in Phil 2:6a and then taking on the "form of a slave" in Phil 2:7b forms a theological parallel to how the process of enslavement was conceived in the surrounding society. Christ is uprooted from the realm where he belongs, where, so to speak, he has natal ties to divinity, and in terms of external reality finds himself in the human realm where he does not belong (schēmati euretheis hōs anthrōpos, v8a). The verb etapeinōsev in v8b both recapitulates the idea of Christ divesting himself of his divinity, which has already been expressed by the phrase "he emptied himself" in v7b, and, more importantly, links Christ's humiliation to his death—"he humbled himself and became obedient unto death." Here one finds the theological echo of the second state of enslavement, the incorporation of the slave into the master's society as a nonbeing, as someone socially dead.

The second set of categories, which one can fruitfully borrow from Patterson, to elucidate the Philippians hymn are the mutually dependent concepts of honor and degradation. These, as Patterson argues, provide the symbolic and psychic framework of a slaveowning society (Patterson:77-101). The social demarcation between free and slave is the boundary between persons with and persons without honor. Indeed, one of the incentives to own slaves is the representation of the master's honor. The sense of honor among the free is nourished by the lack of it, the degradation, which is seen as the essential character of the slave. Honor may be an important idea in a wide range of societies but in slaveowning societies it is central and predominant, they are in the full sense timocratic societies. I have already noted how Philippians emphasizes the degradation of Christ's earthly existence in the form of a slave by comparing it to his prior equality with God and his subsequent elevation to lordship over the cosmos. Philippians integrates the dynamics of honor and degradation, underlying a slaveowning society, into its christology. The paradox is that master and slave are one and the same person. Thus, the honor, which is due Christ as being both equal with God and lord of the cosmos, cannot be separated from the degradation of Christ in the form of a slave. The social differentiation between persons is replaced by a theological distinction between the states of Christ's existence. The honor of Christ's divine pre-existence and final existence as cosmic ruler is not only compared with but is dependent on the degradation of Christ's earthly existence. There is no reason to restrict the conjunction dio in v9a to indicating the death on the cross as the sole reason for God's exaltation of Christ. Rather, God's action appears to be the counterpoint of the whole movement of self-abasement on Christ's part.

At this point, one needs to take account of two distinct ways in which the practices and psychology of ancient slavery have shaped the Philippians text. What action has God found favorable in Christ? It is not the death on the cross *per se* but its context of the obedience which Christ owes God (v8c "obedient unto death, even death on a cross"), God is, therefore, described as having the same expectations of Christ in the form of a slave as a human master had of the slave in the world of the New Testament. In the ancient literature on slavery obedience was considered the chief virtue of the slave, his or her essential characteristic for behavior proper to the slave's status and function (Bradley:33-40). Indeed, apart from or without obedience, and its corollary of loyalty to the master, the slave was usually considered a moral inferior (Wiedemann:61-77). This emphasis on obedience as the primary ethical requirement of the slave is, of course, the content of New Testament moral exhortation to Christian slaves (Ephes 6:5, Col 3:22, Tit 2:9, 1. Pet 2:18). One of the motivations for slave obedience was the prospect of manumission, granted by the master as a reward for good behavior. Yet, God's exaltation of Christ does not resemble a manumission. The status, which Christ attains, is not invested with the same mental structures of dependence and inferiority as the social relationship between freedman and patron. Christ is the ideal slave and his obedience makes him worthy of God's reward, but Christ is essentially not a slave, and, consequently, the end of his enslavement is not a manumission but a restitution of his original glory and honor.

One has recognised a literary and psychological parallel between the Philippians hymn and the basic plot of the Hellenistic novel in their use of the motif of slavery (Hock). In Chariton's *Callirhoe*, Xenophon's *Ephesiaka*, Longus' *Daphnis and Chloë* and Achilles Tatius' *Leukippe and Kleitophon* the story hinges on the enslavement of high-born persons through such misfortunes as capture by pirates or infant exposure, the recognition after many trials of their true identity and their restoration to a status of honor. The characterization of the heroes and heroines of these novels is reminiscent of how Christ is depicted in Philippians. When they are reduced to slavery, they are essentially not slaves, but they do not resist their role as slaves. Instead, they are exemplary in their obedience and their moral superiority to their servile status is expressed not through an attempt to claim the honor, which is intrinsically theirs, but their acquiescence in their conditions of dishonor.

The Social Effects of the Philippians Hymn

Despite the many differences between the Hellenistic novel and the liturgical text of Philippians, the portrayal of Christ, like that of the enslaved heroes and heroines of the romances, contains an idealization of the slave role. One can interpret vv7b and 7c as parallel statements that equate Christ's morphēv doulou labōv with his en homoiōmati anthrōpōn genomenos and conclude that the metaphysical understanding of the human condition as slavery, common to "religious Hellenism" underlies this text (Käsemann:73f.). Nonetheless, the acceptance of slavery as an ineradicable constituent of human society was strengthened rather than diminished by its universalization as metaphor for the human condition. The belief that all human beings are slaves in the metaphysical sense, and that likewise Christ in becoming human took on the slavery of the human condition, does not produce the effect of a social levelling. That all persons are slaves by virtue of their humanity does not preclude that some persons are slaves by virtue of their social status. Indeed, the supposed metaphysical reality of universal human slavery reinforces the social reality of a particular institution of slavery by encouraging endurance of the human condition rather than transformation of it through one's own efforts. Christ in similar fashion to the heroes and heroines of the Hellenistic novel is passive in his delivery from slavery. The rescue from slavery, whether in a fictional, christological or metaphysical setting, depends on the intervention of a higher power. The social forces, which kept the institution of slavery in place, were as opaque to the ancient mind as the metaphysical powers that dominated the universe. One might even hypothesize that the forcefulness of the metaphor of bondage for the human condition derived from the lack of transparency, inherent in the social condition of slavery. Phil 2:6-11 on the metaphorical and theological level was part of a social construction of reality that conveyed the message to those enslaved that opposition to their slavery was as hopeless as resistance to their humanity.

Although there is an idealization of the slave role through the characterization of Christ as the perfectly obedient slave, the identification of Christ with a slave is ruptured in the Philippians text itself. Christ's enslavement diverges from the social reality in a crucial aspect which constituted slavery as slavery in distinction from other forms of human service. Christ's enslavement is voluntary and its quality of free choice is underlined by the linguistically peculiar phrase of v7 "he emptied himself" (eauton ekenōsev). The emphatic use of the reflexive here points out that Christ is not stripped of his original divine honor by God but lays it aside through his own free action. The rejection of the view that Philippians contains the idea of the divine pre-existence of Christ was in part motivated by the desire to see a full identification of the humiliated one with the exalted one (Talbert, Murphy-O'Connor) and to regard the voluntariness of Christ's slave existence as a radical human choice. "Whereas the righteous man in *Wisdom* suffers because there is no alternative, the state in which Christ found himself was freely chosen" (Murphy-O'Connor: 41). Even a defence of the divine pre-existence of Christ in Philippians may wish to stress that the theme of humiliation and subsequent exaltation predominates over that of pre-existence (Wong: 281). Christ's divine pre-existence or prior worth radically differentiates him from other human beings because it enables a *self*-humiliation which they are not capable of. The statement that Christ "emptied himself" may indicate that a divine pre-existence of Christ is according to Philippians not the primary definition of Christ's original status, but that the priority of Christ according to his worth precedes the sense of temporal priority and its ontological implication of pre-existence. Christ's divine priority of worth is seen as confirmed in the paradox of his voluntary renunciation of it. The tension created in the text through the statement that a divine being becomes a slave is relieved through the removal of this christological enslavement from any analogy with an act of human enslavement. The human slave did not choose her or his servile status nor, for that matter, did human beings choose to be born. The total involuntariness of the slave's condition, corresponding to the master's total control of the slave, was fundamental to the social institution and to its adoption as a metaphor for the human condition.

Why was the tension of a divine being becoming a slave relieved? Was the thought of an authentic enslavement of Christ, in which the theological statement fully reduplicated the social reality of slavery, unbearable? Of even greater significance is the question whether the slave and the slaveowner would have found the involuntary taking on the form of a slave by Christ unbearable in the same way. Perhaps, the slave was comforted by the thought that she or he, like Christ, was not in reality a slave and did not, therefore, possess the moral inferiority of the slave, that she or he would be vindicated by God before the cosmos and their honor recognised and restored. Yet, the voluntary servitude of Christ in contrast to the slave's totally involuntary enslavement would have operated as a cognitive check on their full identification with the Christ of the Philippians hymn. From the slaveowner's viewpoint the radical disjunction between Christ taking on the form of a slave and the social process of enslavement meant that the idealization of the role of the slave did not lead to the valorization of the slave. The paradox of someone, indeed a divine being, choosing the degradation of a slave had a potentially scandalizing effect on a slaveowning society. Yet, this was neutralized by Christ depicted as possessing and exercising the very opposite of slavery—freedom.

Christ does not take on the moral inferiority of the slave. Although in v7 humanity itself seems to be viewed as slavery, it is not further equated with sinfulness (Wanamaker:188-89). The theme of human beings as "slaves of sin" was elaborated in Paul's theology and was a common topos in patristic writings. Despite the linguistic parallel between Christ being "born in the likeness of men" (en omoiōmati anthrōpōn genomenos) of v7c and God's sending of his Son "in the likeness of sinful flesh" (en homoiōmati sarkos hamartias) of Rom 8:3, it must be seen as significant that Philippians avoids the statement that Christ's unearthly existence under the conditions of a slave are also under the conditions of sin. The theological metaphor of slavery as sin drew upon the denial of moral autonomy and the attribution of moral inferiority to the slave in antiquity. Philippians is careful to dissociate Christ from the morally defective nature of a slave. Rather, Christ's obedience in his earthly existence makes him the anthropological model of the "slaves of righteousness" (Rom 6:16-18) who are characterized through their obedience to God. Here the conception of Christ as the ideal slave seems to coalesce with and become subordinate to that of the 'ebed Yahweh', the righteous and suffering servant of Isaiah 53 (Lohmeyer:94; Martin:182-90, 195; Hofius:70-73), which underwent further evolution in Wisdom literature (Georgi), or that more general Jewish figure of the righteous and obedient person who suffers for God's sake (Schweizer:135; Kleinknecht:311). The dependence of the Philippians text on the mental universe of slaveholding antiquity is attested not only by what it incorporates of the social reality of slavery into its christological metaphor but also by those elements which it excludes. Hence, precisely at the point where Philippians could have challenged the ethical and anthropological assumptions about the slave, it avoids the question whether slavery is equivalent to moral inferiority.

Analogy and Detecting the Subversion of the Text by the Oppressed

Although the Philippians hymn did not challenge ancient concepts of servile moral nature, neither did it directly affirm them. I am not making an argument from silence with the desperate intent of finding some liberation content in the text. All attempts, including the above, at reconstructing the meaning of a text in the community, which originally produced and performed it, are beset by the dangers of hypothesizing mental processes of those historically removed from us. Yet, there is an even greater danger of limiting such hypotheses to what seems to have objective support in the text itself. The analogy between the unknown of the present and the unknown of the past should heighten the contemporary reader's awareness that possible meanings, given to the text by the oppressed, may be improbable or impossible meanings *in* the text. The text of Phil 2:6-11, as we have it, is kyriocentric. It does not challenge the interests or beliefs of slavemasters. Yet, there is an irreducible tension in the idea of a god who becomes a slave, which cannot be overcome by depicting Christ as simultaneously the ideal and the atypical slave. The identification of Christ with God allowed the enslavement of Christ to be seen as equivalent to the enslavement of God. To be able to think the enslavement of God makes it possible to conceive of an inversion of the hierarchy of being and worth, held in ancient society. The imagination of the slaves in confronting the Philippians hymn was not circumscribed by the logical associations of the text within the dominant symbolic universe, precisely that which is reconstructed by conventional biblical exegesis. The subjectivity which might have been the slaves as they subverted the text of Phil 2:6-11 is not historiographically recoverable. It is a past that can only be invented, a theological task proper to the narrative creativity of biblical proclamation within the communities of the oppressed today.

Although one cannot argue for particular ways in which ancient slaves subverted Phil 2:6-11 and similar texts, one can ascertain the likelihood that such a subversion occurred. It is true that the institution of ancient slavery did not lead to an abolitionist movement, and that the existing social order without slavery seemed inconceivable to both free and slave. Nonetheless, the existing social order was relativized in myth and religion. One could think of an original Golden Age as a world without slavery and some Christians believed that the new existence, obtained for them through Christ's death and resurrection and their incorporation into Christ by baptism, was one in which the distinction between slave and free no longer pertained (Gal 3:28). Stoics, Cynics and Christians taught that freedom was essentially an inner quality rather than an external social status, although such opinions tended to bolster rather than damage the social institution (Finley:120-

22). The frequent admonitions of slaves to obedience in the New Testament are more likely to indicate that Christian slaves were prone to insubordination than to exemplary docility. Slave rebellions, however rare, did occur (Wiedemann:198-223) and everyday acts of resistance by slaves to their servitude, such as stealing, poor and slow work performance, led to the slaveowner's insistence on loyalty and obedience (Bradley:28-33).

However ineradicable the institution of slavery may have seemed, those who were enslaved did not wish to remain slaves and it was taken for granted by ancient writers that the slave longed for freedom. Despite its opaqueness and aura of inevitability the ancient institution of slavery rested on an elaborate system of social control. The methods by which masters maintained their domination over their slaves ranged from overt brutality to the more "humane" treatment of offering their slaves such incentives as the hope of manumission. Yet, such social control did not automatically produce social harmony. Tacitus (*Annals* 14.42-5) recounts the execution in 61 C.E. of four hundred slaves, including women and children, because one of their number had murdered their master. This was the penalty prescribed by Roman law for all slaves in a household where a master was murdered. The implementation of such severe legislation in the New Testament period shows that the social conflicts, inherent in a slave society, were in the final instance only contained by the exercise and threat of violence against the enslaved.

There is no evidence that Christianity attracted a class of slaves, peculiarly contented with their fate. Even if they were not rebellious or unduly recalcitrant they would not have escaped from the permanent tension between slave and master. By making a careful analogy between the ancient slave-master relationship and other social relationships between oppressor and oppressed, one can avoid some false assumptions. That the early Christian community contained both slaves and slaveholders does not imply an unusual level of social cohesion between master and slave. There were no slave cults in the Greco-Roman world and slaves participated in the same religions as their owners. Yet, common religious beliefs and practices do not necessarily defuse social conflict. In the American Old South slaves and masters often shared the same evangelical faith, and in present-day Latin America the élites and the impoverished masses often practice the same form of Catholicism. In both cases one could not easily detect obvious and apparent social protest in the religious expressions of the oppressed. Yet, it would be grossly misleading to claim that unless an Afro-American evangelical slave espoused the religiously motivated abolitionist views of Daniel Alexander Payne and unless a Catholic Latin American peasant advocates the liberation theology of Gustavo Gutiérrez that their respective religiosity is a form of acquiescence in their oppression. We do not have for antiquity an abundant documentation of folk religion nor a living oral tradition, which in the modern examples allows us to see the elements of resistance to oppression in the apparently innocuous religiosity of the oppressed. It seems more credible to believe that such elements were present rather than not in the religious experience of Greco-Roman slaves. Wherever relationships of great disparity in social power exist, social conflict will be generated. It seems likely that such social conflict was felt by the slaves in the early Christian community and that this shaped the meanings, however irretrievable, which they invested in the common religious expressions of the early church.

I hope I have demonstrated the significance of the use of analogy in a hermeneutics which can probe beyond the structures of oppression, embedded in a text, to the possibilities of liberation not given by the text but claimed from it by the oppressed.

WORKS CONSULTED

Bradley, K.R.
    1984   *Slaves and Masters in the Roman Empire. A Study in Social Control.* Collection Latomus, 185. Brussels: Latomus, Revue d'Études Latines.

Finley, M.I.
    1980   *Ancient Slavery and Modern Ideology.* New York: the Viking Press.

Georgi, Dieter
    1964   "Der vorpaulinische Hymnus Phil 2, 6-11." Pp. 263-93 in *Zeit und Geschicte. Dankesqabe an Rudolf Bultmann zum 80. Geburtstag.* Ed. Erich Dinkler. Tübingen: J.C.B. Mohr (Paul Siebeck).

Hock, Ronald P.
    forthcoming   "Christology and the Conventions of Ancient Slavery: Looking Again at Phil. 2:5-11." JBL.

Hofius, Otfried.
    1976   *Der Christushymnus Philipper 2, 6-11.* Wissenschafliche Untersuchungen zum Neuen Testament 17. Tübingen: J.C.B. Mohr (Paul Siebeck).

Käsemann, Ernst
1960   "Kritische Analyse von Phil. 2, 5-11" *Exegetische Versuche und Besinnungen*, I. Göttingen: Vandenhoeck & Ruprecht.

Kleinknecht, Karl Theodor
1984   *Der leidende Gerectfertigte. Die alttestamentlich-jüdische Tradition vom "leidenden Gerechten" und ihre Rezeption bei Paulus*. Wissenschaftliche Untersuchungen zum Neuen Testament, 2. Reihe, 13. Tübingen: J.C.B. Mohr (Paul Siebeck).

Lohmeyer, Ernst
1974   *Der Brief an die Philipper*. Göttingen: Vanden hoeck & Ruprecht.

Martin, Ralph P.
1983   *Carmen Christi. Philippians 2:5-11 in Recent Interpretation and in the Setting of Christian Worship*. Rev. ed. Grand Rapids: Wm. B. Eerdmans.

Murphy-O'Connor, Jerome
1976   "Christological Anthropology in Phil. II, 6-11." *RB* 83:25-50.

Patterson, Orlando
1982   *Slavery and Social Death, A Comparative Study*. Cambridge, Mass.: Harvard University Press.

Schüssler Fiorenza, Elisabeth
1983   *In Memory of Her. A Feminist Theological Reconstruction of Christian Origins*. New York: Crossroad.

Schweizer, E.
1962   *Erniedrigung und Erhöhung bei Jesus und seinen Nachfolgern*. ATANT 28. 2nd ed. Zürich: Zwingli.

Talbert, C.H.
1967   "The Problem of Pre-Existence in Philippians 2:6-11." *JBL* 86:141-53.

Wanamaker, C.A.
1987   "Philippians 2.6-11: Son of God or Adamic Christology." *NTS* 33:179-93.

Wiedemann, Thomas
1981   *Greek and Roman Slavery*. London: Crrom Helm.

Wong, Teresia Yai-Chow
1986 "The Problem of Pre-Existence in Philippians 2, 6-11." *ETL* 62:267-82.

www.ingramcontent.com/pod-product-compliance
Lightning Source LLC
Chambersburg PA
CBHW021811220426
43662CB00006B/273